BREAKING BITCH:

DISMANTLING THE *LIES* TO RECLAIM YOUR *TRUTH*

J. R. Baker-Flowers

The UNLEARNing Project® LLC
Publishing

Copyright © 2017 by Jamekaa Richelle Baker-Flowers,
Founder & Creator of The UNLEARNing Project® LLC and Founder, Creator and Producer of The Goddess Unbound: No BITCH Here Project©

All rights reserved. No part of this publication may be reproduced, distributed or transmitted in any form or by any means, including photocopying, recording, or other electronic or mechanical methods, without the prior written permission of the publisher, except in the case of brief quotations embodied in critical reviews and certain other noncommercial uses permitted by copyright law. For permission requests, write to the publisher, addressed "Attention: Permissions Coordinator," at the email address below:

Jamekaa Richelle Baker-Flowers
info@theunlearningproject.org

Indexer: J.R. Baker-Flowers
Cover design: J. R. Baker-Flowers and Karen Ayers, Karen Ayers Design
Edited by J. R. Baker-Flowers, Co-edited by Grace Brown
Appendix research: Beverly Jean Baker-Flowers

The brief lyrics quoted from various musical artists, in addition to the briefly quoted lines from television shows and films are permissible through "fair use" and have been used solely to provide educational and critical commentary.

Book Layout ©2017 https://www.bookdesigntemplates.com

Ordering Information:
Quantity sales. Special discounts are available on quantity purchases by corporations, associations, and others. For details, contact J.R. Baker-Flowers at the email address above.

BREAKING BITCH: Dismantling the LIES to Reclaim Your TRUTH/ J.R. Baker-Flowers. —1st ed.
ISBN: 978-0-692-94075-4

Publisher: The UNLEARNing Project®, LLC
Jamekaa Richelle Baker-Flowers, Founder and Creator

Contents

Introduction 7

Part 1: THE BREAK-DOWN

1 Fractured Society 16
    Media Consumption 23
    The Bitch Narrative in Film and Television 24
    The Bitch Narrative in Music 37
    The Bitch Narrative in Books, Clothing and Alcohol 39

2 Piercing the Shell: Bitch: The Chicken or the Egg Phenomenon 41
    Macro Systems 42
        Patriarchal Ideologies 43
        Media 45
        Capitalist Sexism 47
        Street Harassment 49

    Micro Systems 52
        Individual Attitudes and Belief Systems 53
        Street Harassment 59
        Personal Purchasing Power (PPP©) 62

3 Cracking the Code: Words DO Mean Things 68
    History of "Bitch": Definition and Cultural Origins 71

4 Shattering the Illusions: Breaking Bitch Down!........ 76

    Deconstructing a Social Construct 78
    Reappropriation: The False Tool of Power 81

Part 2: THE BREAKTHROUGH

5 Breaking Free: Your Words Create and Define Your World 86

    Understanding the Power of Language 88

6 Breaking-up with Bitch 102

    Reclaiming Your Truth: A New Era 103

- <u>Activity 1</u>: 5-Step Program to Reclaim, Resurrect and Return to You 107
- <u>Activity 2</u>: 14-Day "I Am" Affirmation Challenge 151

7 Final Remarks 154

Appendix 156

Bibliography 161

Index... 167

About the Author 172

Dedication

To the spirit born in me that recognized its purpose and answered its calling eons ago,

To the fire within me that rages against society's ills and injustices and whose light never extinguishes,

To my ancestors whose voices guide me and whose strength lives through me,

To my radiant, strong and powerful mother whose pure love, undying support and true friendship encourages me to be the light I was born to be,

To my beloved father whose love continues to embrace, protect and watch over me from the eternal beyond,

To my dynamic sisters, my first best-friends, whose humor, love and wit keep me both lifted and grounded

To my love, my cosmic gift, my partner in life, my best-friend and my confidant who inspired me to author this book and encouraged me to share my message with the world,

To my hope and belief in humanity's return to its truth,

"Three things cannot be long hidden: the sun, the moon, and the truth." - Buddha

Ms. Lynda,

Thank you for your Beauty, for your light and your glow!

J.R Baker-Flowers R-

BREAKING BITCH:

Dismantling the LIES to Reclaim Your TRUTH

INTRODUCTION

She watched in horror, endless scenes of women throwing drinks in each other's faces as violently as they threw the term 'bitch' in each other's direction. Surfing between a limitless sea of channels, she felt nauseous from riding the perilous waves of women being displayed as "cutthroat bitches," "uppity bitches," "ambitious bitches," "overly aggressive bitches," "hormonal bitches," and the ever-so modern term "Bad Bitches."

All day, she looked forward to escaping the pangs of another stressful day, where she could enjoy her favorite pastime of watching a little television. That joy ruined, she wondered, 'Is THIS how they view us...as bitches?!" As she gazed upon the 52" flat screen in her living room, she thought back to her experiences earlier that day while in between meetings, walking down the street. Within one hour, she was both directly assaulted by the word "bitch" having been called one as she ignored the sexual advances of "Joe Asshole" on the street, and also disheartened by the word when she overheard two women who, appeared to be friends, call each other bitches "jokingly" while sitting outside having lunch.

Her attention brought back to the present quickly by a rather loud and obnoxious commercial for Viagra single packs, she couldn't help but wonder, "how and when did we become 'bitches' and why is this so acceptable?"

Does this story sound or feel familiar to you? Have you ever experienced a moment in your life where you felt the way the woman in the story did...deeply disheartened, confused or angry by a social issue that affects your or another community's identity and representation? Well, this story accurately reflects the common experiences and thoughts of hundreds of thousands of women in our society that have grown concerned, irate, despondent and utterly exhausted with the repressive and narrow representations, or more appropriately, *misrepresentations*, of women in media, particularly regarding the prevalent moniker "bitch" and how virtually every woman is called one.

As a woman, it has been quite painful and equally upsetting to witness the growing pandemic that is the "culture of bitch." It's everywhere and this term, [which by the way is a slur and has origins rooted in the subjugation of women,] has become one of *the* most acceptable slurs in our society!

Have *you* noticed this? Have *you* noticed how frequently the word "bitch" is used in your favorite television shows? Have *you* recognized how female characters in these and other television programs, as well as films are called "bitches," by both male *and* female characters substantially more than male characters are called a specific gender-based slur? Come to think of it, *is* there a gender-based slur or collective derogatory term for men? Have *you* noticed the meteoric rise of "reality TV shows" and the almost requisite usage of the word "bitch" when female characters are strategically placed...excuse me, "captured" in these fist fighting, drink slinging brawls? What about the current, widely used "progressive spin" on the term, "bitch," as in *"bad bitch?"* Have *you* observed how embracing our society has become of this pseudo-empowering term? It's as if placing the word "bad" before "bitch" magically negates the definition and energetic meaning of this oppressively dehumanizing word!

Some women even wear it with pride on their clothing as a "badge of honor" and also place the hashtag *"#badbitch"* as a digital signature on their social media personas. Finally, have *you* witnessed the countless young girls and teenagers casually using this term as a fundamental source of their identities?

The word "bitch," a gender-based slur and derogatory term in its truest nature, is literally **EVERYWHERE** and has become a centralized fixture of our society woven into the very fabric of our socio-ideological framework. Yet, in spite of the many recent sociopolitical shifts in our global society to redress longstanding systemic injustices, (i.e. Black Lives Matter to address systemic racial injustices, the Equal Pay Act to address gender wage inequities, the Marriage Equality Act to legalize marriage for LGBTQ civil rights, etc.,) the overwhelming prevalence and presence of the word "bitch" existing in our society has been ignored and overlooked. Moreover, because this word is rooted in misogyny, patriarchy and sexism, this begs the question, *"Why hasn't this issue been brought to the forefront of discussion for social transformation?"*

Many would make the hackneyed and overused argument of "freedom of speech" in response to the above question and also contend that people should be allowed to say whatever they feel. This includes calling someone or an entire group a defamatory name essentially because *"you can."* Furthermore, because we live in a westernized and therefore, egoistic society, we have literally been programmed and conditioned to view the issue of slurs, like "bitch," as innocuous or "just a word." But unfortunately, as a result of this thought process, we have become detached from the reality of personal accountability and the outcomes or inevitable consequences that ensue after using this kind of dehumanizing language.

It has become painfully apparent that this "pass the buck," unconcerned, #idgaf (*I don't give a fuck*) mentality has not exactly served our society well, evident by the current state we are in, which is illustrated by: a) the sexist and patriarchal representation of women in media, b) the capitalist exploitation of the word "bitch" to further the perpetuation of a misogynistic ethos, c) incessant occurrences of Street Harassment and the resulting violence towards women and d) the rising campaign to coax women into embracing or "reappropriating" the word "bitch" as a term of endearment or empowerment. *This* is the current state of our society! And for these and countless other reasons, which I will speak to throughout this book, it is vital to our very humanity and the propagation of our future existence that we *must* divorce ourselves from this "culture of bitch" and return to our truth!

Given the topic of this book, many will automatically make sweeping assumptions and generalizations about the intention(s) of this text. With that, allow me to explain what this book is not: *BREAKING BITCH: Dismantling the LIES to Reclaim Your TRUTH* is not a man-hating, male-bashing manifesto, where men are depicted as "the enemy" or "the source" of the problem that is the "culture of bitch." Men as a group have, unfortunately, been the originators and benefactors of the term's usage as a patriarchal, social and political construct, as well as a sexist institution. However, men, just as women, have been *taught* and socialized to adopt or internalize this sexist ideology; for they [men] did not emerge from their mother's wombs into existence with an innately "anti-woman" mentality, but have been wholly conditioned and molded by this widespread cultural ethos.

BREAKING BITCH: Dismantling the LIES to Reclaim Your TRUTH is not the newest self help or self-empowerment book SOLELY marketed to women, young adult females and teenage girls. This book will not initially claim to empower the entire community of women only to identify them as the scapegoat responsible for perpetuating the term "bitch" simply because a few women advocate for the approach to "reappropriate" the term. In this contemporary era, many place blame on women for this term's existence stating, "*if women didn't call themselves or other women 'bitches,' men wouldn't use the term and it would no longer exist.*" This form of "blame the victim," moronic finger pointing is as logical as the African-American/Black identified community being blamed as *THE* cause or *THE* problem why the "N-word" is still present and prevalent!

BREAKING BITCH: Dismantling the LIES to Reclaim Your TRUTH is not the newest item in sensationalized media to place blame on celebrities and celebrity culture for being *THE* reason or sole contributing factor for the perpetuation of the "culture of bitch." The celebrities (i.e. musicians, actors, film and television writers and producers,) mentioned in this book are referenced as mere examples of how diverse conduits and members of media participate in this growing sociopolitical and cultural phenomenon.

Finally, this book, *BREAKING BITCH: Dismantling the LIES to Reclaim Your TRUTH,* has not been written and published to achieve punitive, finger pointing measures in making those that use the word "bitch," in any capacity, feel shunned or ashamed. Playing the blame-game achieves absolutely nothing and further separates a society already broken. You see, this book has been written to draw attention to the monolithic crises that is ironically everywhere and impacts virtually every area of our society and lives, yet is and has been overlooked and is not talked about.

Now, let me tell you what this book *is* about: If you have ever, even once, questioned the excessive presence of the word "bitch" or the increasing socio-systemic visibility of the term "bad bitch," then this book is for you! If you've ever been called a "bitch" or witnessed someone being called one, this book is for you! If you've watched a television program or film and 1) noticed the frequent times female characters were called "bitches," and 2) became angry or upset as a result, this book is for you! If you use or have used the word "bitch" unapologetically, describing yourself or another person, then this book is for you! If you've used "bitch" or "bad bitch" as a term of empowerment or endearment verbally or electronically in a hashtag or social media post, then this book is for you! If you are on a path of self-liberation and no longer want to be controlled, manipulated or programmed by a global capitalist political economic regime, this book is for you!

In Part 1, *THE BREAK-DOWN* of this book, *BREAKING BITCH: Dismantling the LIES to Reclaim Your TRUTH,* the purpose is to shed light on the crisis that is the "culture of bitch" and why it is a new age system of oppression designed to keep women and men in ideological slavery. This book will unearth the root causes of this widespread problem and analyze the conjoined macro-micro interrelationship (i.e. systemic sexism-individual attitudes,) that perpetuates the "culture of bitch" and moreover, address why abolishing this word from a) our socio-cultural institutions (i.e. media,) b) the capitalist political economy (i.e. commodities, goods and apparel) and c) our personal usage (i.e. conversations with and/or about women and personal identity titles) will lead to the overthrowing of systemic patriarchy and ultimately, the liberation of women, men and our society at-large.

An additional mission of *BREAKING BITCH: Dismantling the LIES to Reclaim Your TRUTH* is to provide an accurate definition of the word "bitch" from a historical analysis, revealing the etymology of this term. Far too often, we use terms, phrases and even practice holidays from a place of ignorance, never asking the questions, *"How did this come into existence?"* or *"What is the meaning of this?"* Just take an informal poll asking people the definition of the word "bitch" and you will hear nearly 15 different contradicting and polarizing definitions ranging from a "strong, cut-throat woman," to "an angry, annoying or nagging woman." Furthermore, this book will address the fundamentally flawed system of "reappropriation" as it relates to the term "bitch." Due to eons of sexist tyranny, many women have declared the need to withdraw the patriarchal power from their male counterparts by redefining the word "bitch" as a term of empowerment. While the intention is understandable, when we truly grasp the accurate meanings and origins of words and in this regard, slurs, we recognize that the concept of "reappropriation" is an inherently destructive tactic to the person or group seeking to "reclaim" the slur and bestows a false sense of power. Think about it. Can a group *truly* reclaim a system or tool of hatred that was *intentionally* created to subjugate them? This further supports the mission of this book to raise consciousness, incite action and propel liberation to deeply examine the nature of "reappropriation," rather than readily adopting it. Knowledge is power after all!

Part 2 of this book, *THE BREAKTHROUGH,* will address the power of language and how the vibrational quality of our words emit frequencies into our vibrational universe that in turn, literally shapes and creates our realities. We've all heard many sayings in the vein of *"your thoughts become your words and your words become your actions"* or *"the tongue is mightier than the sword."* In essence, these adages speak to the concept of energy. Energy is *the* source of creation itself [1]. The universe our planet resides in, the earth and all of her powerful resources, as well as light, electricity, the elements of heat, wind and water, the beating of a heart, laughter, sadness, anger, joy and love, each of these are forms of energy and as we are comprised of a) the identical elements from nature (i.e. the earth) and b) the universe (i.e. star dust,) as well as experience the aforementioned emotions, we ourselves are thus, pure energy! Therefore, we are energetic creators and what we create, which includes what we say, write, print, etc., influences the communities, societies and world we live in.

Finally, this book will encourage you to reclaim your truth and authentic identity through two introspective-mindfulness activities: ACTIVITY 1: a 5-step Program to support you on your journey to reclaiming your truth and ACTIVITY 2: a 14-day "I Am Affirmation Challenge." The ultimate purpose of *BREAKING BITCH: Dismantling the LIES to Reclaim Your TRUTH* is to raise awareness about the unspoken crisis that is the "culture of bitch" and how millions of people have both unconsciously participated in and been victimized by it.

When our ancestors raised their collective voices and shouted *"NO!,"* fighting boldly against many forms of systemic tyranny in the past, they recognized that the system of oppression they were forced into was *not* their truth, but a man-made cage that could be dismantled. We must now raise *our* voices in unity to shout *"NO!"* against this "culture of bitch" that has corrupted and silenced our inherent power.

Welcome to a new era. Welcome to the real you.

Welcome to truth!

PART 1:
THE BREAK-DOWN

CHAPTER 1

Fractured Society: Culture of Bitch

In an automated voice, *"BEEP!" "BEEP!" BEEP! We interrupt your regularly scheduled program to present all of your favorite entertainment. Don't be alarmed...they all contain the word 'BITCH!'"*

"Sit back, relax and enjoy!

Reality TV

The Real Housewives of Atlanta
The Real Housewives of Orange County
The Real Housewives of Beverly Hills
The Real Housewives of New Jersey
The Real Housewives of New York
Love and Hip Hop: LA
Love and Hip Hop: Hollywood
Love and Hip Hop: Atlanta
The Bad Girls Club
Little Women: Atlanta
Little Women: Dallas

Mob Wives

Television Programs

Scandal
How to Get Away With Murder
American Horror Story
Empire
Archer
Brickleberry
Insecure
True Blood
Banshee
Sex and the City
The Office
Parks and Recreation
Dexter
Grace and Frankie
The Mick
Dish Nation
The Get Down
Blindspot
Chicago Justice
The Catch
Shades of Blue
Saturday Night Live
Greenleaf
Goliath
The Boondocks
Big Little Lies
Ozark
Stranger Things
Jessica Jones
The Deuce
Orphan Black
The Orville
The Five
This Is Us

Big Mouth
Schitt's Creek
MINDHUNTER
Slasher
London Spy
The Punisher
Scream Queens
She's Gotta Have It (2017)
The Climb
The Marvelous Mrs. Maisel
The Magicians
13 Reasons Why
Mosaic

Movies

Sisters
Bitch
Bridesmaids
Mean Girls
Dolores Claibourne
Transformers: Revenge of the Fallen
Transformers: The Last Knight
The Boss
Get Out
Snatched
Gone Girl
Suicide Squad
Forrest Gump
Run Bitch Run
Pulp Fiction
Skyfall
Equalizer
Rush Hour 2
XXX
Friday
Next Friday
Friday After Next

All About the Benjamins
Kong: Skull Island
Chronicles of Riddick
Be Cool
Message from the King
Independence Day: Resurgence
Live Free or Die Hard
Torque
Baby Driver
The Belko Experiment
Atomic Blonde
Collateral Beauty
The Hitman's Bodyguard
What Happened to Monday?
Kingsman: The Golden Circle
The Hunter's Prayer
Girl's Trip
Baywatch
Wanted
Going In Style
Three Billboards Outside Ebbing, Missouri
Batman V Superman: Dawn of Justice
Wheelman
Thor: Ragnarok
The Adjustment Bureau
Die Another Day
The Last Word
Big Fish
Little Bitches
The Dressmaker
Salmon Fishing In Yemen
Kiss Kiss Bang Bang
Proud Mary

Music

"Bitch Better Have My Money" by Rihanna
"Work Bitch" by Britney Spears

"Bad Bitch" by French Montana
"Good Weed Bad Bitch" by K Camp
"Flawless" by Beyoncè
"That's My Bitch" by Jay-Z and Kanye West
"I'm a Bitch" by Meredith Brooks
"The Makings of a Perfect Bitch" by Nas
"Me & My Bitch" by Biggie
"Sophisticated Bitch" by Public Enemy
"Wonda Why They Call U Bitch" by 2Pac
"Anaconda," by Nicki Minaj
"I'm Legit" by Nicki Minaj
"Perfect Bitch" by Kanye West
"Bitch Don't Kill My Vibe," by Kendrick Lamar
"Keeps Gettin' Better" by Christina Aguilera
"Crazy Bitch" by Buckcherry
"Bad Bitch" by Bebe Rexha feat. Ty Dolla $ign

Books

"How to Be A Bad Bitch," by Amber Rose
"Bitch Series," by Joy Deja King
"Why Men Love Bitches," by Sherry Argov
"Boss Bitch: A Simple 12-Step Plan to Take Charge of Your Career," by Nicole Lapin
"Skinny Bitch," by Rory Freedman and Kim Barnouin
"Getting in Touch with Your Inner Bitch," by Elizabeth Hilts
"Bitch Doctrine," by Laurie Penny
"The Bitch," by Jackie Collins
"The Bitch is in The House," by Cathi Hanauer
"Switch the Bitch," by Pettifleur Berenger
"The Bitch Switch," by Omarosa Manigualt
"Good Christian Bitches," by Kim Gatlin
"Bitch Are You Retarded? Stop Being A Dumbass Either He Loves You, He's in Love with You, or You're Just Something to Do for Right Now. Either Way, Learn the Difference, and When to Walk Away," by Carlos J. Lee

Alcohol, Food and Clothing Commodities

Bitch Vodka
Bitch Wine
Raging Bitch Ale
Bitchin Sauce
Bad Bitches Clothing
Bad Bitches Link Up by Caviar Blaque Apparel
onebadbitch.com
Skinny Bitch Apparel
http://www.bitchplz.org
Thunderbitch
www.sledbitch.com
Bad Bitch Empire (https://www.houseofmoira.com)
The Bitch Bible
Sweet Bitch

Social Media

Instagram, Facebook, Twitter, Snapchat, http://thebitchybible.com, Tumblr, etc. via "Bitches Be Like" memes

It's everywhere! Surrounding you. Infiltrating your mind. Whispering in your ears. Splashed all over the pages of your favorite magazine or blog. Echoing loudly from your beloved television shows and films. Dancing across your body from your favorite clothing. Floating through the ethers of space, imprinting on the innocent minds of your children. "BITCH!" Everywhere you look, the word is there. Hard to miss, like the towering skyscrapers in New York, like the never-ending sea of cars on the highway during rush hour, or the amusement park line of customers waiting to enter the department stores on Black Friday or...racism. It's everywhere! Yet, while these societal fixtures are difficult to ignore, they've become so normalized in our society that we only look upon these phenomena, but don't actually *see* them. Thus, they have become virtually invisible or obscure to our mind's eye. "Bitch" has become one of these commonplace social fixtures.

This single word, ["bitch,"] has permeated virtually every structure that has shaped and influenced our society. Think about it. What are the most prominent infrastructures in our world? They are a) Media (i.e. television, films, news, music, social networks and books,) b) Commodities (i.e. food, fashion, alcohol/liquor, etc.,) c) Religion and d) Government. Reflect for a moment on the way(s) in which you spend the majority of your time. When you think of your favorite pastime or hobby, what activity or activities do you participate in? When you're on your way to and from work, what activity do you engage in to make your commute more pleasant? When you want to relax or spend time with yourself, what fills your time? When you want to celebrate a happy moment in your life, what's one of the first celebratory acts you think of?

By now, you've responded to these questions with activities including, watching television, going to the movies or streaming films online, listening to your favorite music, favorite podcast or a popular audiobook, reading a great novel, posting selfies to your favorite social media site or trolling twitter for comedic content, buying a new outfit, wardrobe or those shoes you've been eyeing for a while now and/or going out for a drink, or many, with your friends. The primary activities or hobbies most of us partake in are largely relegated to the spheres of media and commodities. Moreover, it's reflective of how fundamental and centralized these pastimes have become to our daily experiences and illustrates just how strongly we rely on and *consume* diverse media and commodities.

Media Consumption

What's the best way to disseminate a message, campaign or viewpoint? The answer is MEDIA! Let's take stock for a moment:

- ❖ Within this technocratic society, the average North American spends over 5.11 hours watching television; 99 percent of homes own at least one television set with the average number being over two TV sets; 6 million videos are rented daily in the United States and 1,480 minutes or 24.66667 hours per week the average child watches television[2].

- ❖ In 2015, the *Pew Research Center* conducted a study which found that 45 percent of U.S. adults own a tablet, while 68 percent of adults within the U.S. own a smartphone[3].

- ❖ In 2016, *Brandwatch* reported that of the 3.17 billion Internet users, on average, they have 5.54 social media accounts. There are 2.3 billion active users on social media with 12 new social media mobile users each second. These avid social media users frequent sites including *Facebook* (1.71 billion users with 8 billion average daily video views from 500 million users,) *Twitter* (320 million users,) Instagram (400 million users,) *Snapchat* (100 million users who view 6 billion videos daily,) *WhatsApp* (900 million users) and *YouTube* (over 1 billion users.) *Google* alone comprises 89.3 percent of all the Internet searches with an average of 40,000 searches every second[4].

The "Bitch" Narrative in Television and Film

Regarding our voracious consumption of television, reality TV has become *the* leading program genre over the last 20 years. Within the last decade, the number of Real Housewives and other woman-centered lifestyle Reality TV shows has all but dominated television programming, with sitcoms and dramas following behind. Consider the overwhelming number of TV shows in this voyeuristic genre:

The Real Housewives Genus

Domestic:
The Real Housewives of Orange County
The Real Housewives of New York City
The Real Housewives of Atlanta
The Real Housewives of New Jersey
The Real Housewives of D.C.
The Real Housewives of Beverly Hills
The Real Housewives of Miami
The Real Housewives of Potomac
The Real Housewives of Dallas

International:
The Real Housewives of Athens
The Real Housewives of Vancouver
Les Vraies Housewives (France)
The Real Housewives of Cheshire
The Real Housewives of Auckland
The Real Housewives of Sydney
The Real Housewives of Toronto

The Real Housewives of Melbourne

The Real Housewives Spinoffs

Date My Ex: Jo & Slade
Kandi's Wedding
Bethenny Ever After
Manzo'd with Children
Don't Be Tardy for the Party
Kandi's Ski Trip
Havana Elsa
Teresa Checks In
The Kandi Factory
Vanderpump Rules
Vanderpump Rules After Show
Tamra's OC Wedding
I Dream of NeNe: The Wedding

The Socialite, Wives, Fiancé, Girlfriend and "Other" Genus

Basketball Wives LA
Basketball Wives Miami
Mob Wives Staten Island
Mob Wives Chicago
Love and Hip Hop: LA

Love and Hip Hop: Atlanta
Love and Hip Hop: New York
Love and Hip Hop: Hollywood
Little Women: LA
Little Women: Atlanta

The number of television programs within this voyeuristic, "behind the scenes," glimpse into the lives of "the other half" genre is quite staggering. What's more jarring is the number of times the word "bitch" is uttered from the cast members on each of these shows consistently. It's almost as if it were written into the script! (Pause to let my sarcastic tone to take effect.) One of the most enticing qualities of this genre of Reality TV are the perfectly orchestrated innumerable brawls featuring recurring cast members and "special guests" engaging in incessant arguments and gossip, throwing drinks and other objects at each other's faces, as well as taking part in fist fights all while calling each other *"bitches."*

While many argue that these shows are merely for "entertainment" and captures the "real lives" of these women, the larger issue is the capitalist-systemic perpetuation of archaic stereotypes of women, which are rooted in sexism, patriarchy and misogyny. Each of the previously mentioned woman-centered Reality TV shows are built on an overarching ethos of these women as "appealing" only due to whom they're married or engaged to or dating, as well as their personas being as extravagant, superficial, materialistic, "catty" and as vapid as their lifestyles!

One may pose the question, *"Why do these women act in this manner?,"* when the question that should be asked is, *"Why do television production companies and their parent corporations continue to create, produce and distribute content that propagates these harmful, anti-woman stereotypes?"* Bravotv.com reports that its programming reaches 3.9 million people monthly within the United States, accounting for 85 percent of their global audience. 153.7 million views in the U.S. take place on viewers' mobile devices versus the 137.6 million views occurring on desktops[5]. Translation: That's a whole lot of *"bitches"* and anti-woman stereotypes being manufactured, produced, marketed and consumed!

In regards to scripted television shows, including dramas and sitcoms, the word "bitch" has become a standard fixture in this genre as well. Television programs, like *Don't Trust the B**** In Apartment 23,* centered on the concept of a naïve and bright-eyed, blonde-haired young woman not being able to trust the dark-haired, "wild" new roommate with whom she finds herself sharing an apartment. The popular NBC show *Heroes,* created in 2006 by Tim Kring, featured the leading female characters being called "bitch" or "bitchy" 10 times within the first 9 episodes of Season 1. In *American Horror Story,* created by Ryan Murphy and Brad Falchuck, the word "bitch," uttered primarily to and about women, is said dozens of times throughout each of the highly popular seasons, specifically in seasons 1-5. In *American Horror Story: Coven,* the very first episode is named *"Bitchcraft"* and throughout the entire 13-episode season, the women in the show use the term to refer to one another as "bitch" a total of 46 times. Other variations of this term, including "son of a bitch" and "bitch-slapped," are used twice.

Sex and the City, another television program that has heavily influenced popular culture, featured the female foursome referring to themselves and other women as "bitches" frequently throughout the six-season series. Famous lines from the characters on the show are:

> ❖ *"Okay, I'm a bitch, I'm sorry."* and *"I'm your booth bitch."* - Carrie Bradshaw speaking to Aiden
>
> ❖ *"Don't be a bitch."* -Mr. Big *"I'm not, I'm being myself."* - Carrie
>
> ❖ *"If I worried what every bitch in New York was saying about me, I'd never leave the house."* – Samantha
>
> ❖ *"She stole my baby name!" "You Bitch!"* - Charlotte and Samantha speaking to their former friend Laney respectively.

The incredibly popular ABC television show, *How to Get Away With Murder,* created by Peter Nowalk and housed under Shonda Rhimes' production company *Shondaland,* uses the word "bitch" quite frequently throughout the series. The term is used consistently in a pejorative manner and is also used as a situational point of reference in the following ways:

> ➢ man-to-woman: *"stop acting like a little bitch baby.,"* Connor talking to Michaela in Season 1 Episode 1

- man-to-person on telephone: *"We are open for business and the market is kissing 17 again, you punk ass bitch.,"* Stock broker speaking on the hands-free phone to a client with Wes in his office in Season 1 Episode 4

- man-to-man: *"don't be a bitch.,"* Oliver to Connor in Season 1 Episode 4

- male-to-group: *"are you bitches seriously trying to ignore me right now?,"* Asher shouting to Wes, Michaela, Connor and Laurel hiding in the Keating Law Firm and home in Season 1 Episode 4

- woman-about-man: *"Our whole case just got thrown out. Ryan's going to prison for the rest of his life where he will probably become somebody's bitch boy.,"* Laurel speaking to Frank about their client Ryan in Season 1 Episode 5

- man-referencing-another man's statement: *"All cop killers deserve to fry. Especially little bitches who don't know how to respect their daddy.,"* Judge reading juror's biased statement from "Humper" the dating app in Season 1 Episode 5

- woman-to-man: *"Bitch please!,"* Bonnie speaking to Frank about his leering at Laurel in Season 1 Episode 5

- male-to-male-about-woman: *"bitches be crazy!,"* Connor says to Wes about Rebecca Sutter, their client and Wes' girlfriend in Season 1 Episode 8

- woman-to-woman: *"you sign or I will make sure that you go back to that nasty, backwood, bayou swamp you came from you stubborn bitch!,"* Mrs. Walker,

Michaela's future mother-in-law, says threateningly to Michaela after she protests signing the prenuptial agreement in Season 1 Episode 8

➢ man-about-woman: *"Mr. Smalley, is it true your ex-girlfriend took care of you during your hospital stay?" "Rosalyn? Yeah, but don't believe anything that bitch says."* Mr. Smalley, a witness in a case, says to Bonnie as she questions him in court in Season 1 Episode 13

➢ woman-to-woman: *"I'm not afraid to hit a bitch!,"* Michaela to Laurel in Season 2 Episode 1

➢ man-about-woman: *"That bitch.,"* Victor Lesher says about Annalise to his clients Caleb and Catherine Hapstall when he discovers she has set him up in Season 2 Episode 1

➢ woman-to-woman: *"ok, who is this bitch?!,"* female investigator and friend of Frank speaking about and to Laurel in Season 2 Episode 2

➢ female teenager-to-female teenager: *"YOU'RE A LIAR! YOU WERE NOTHING UNTIL YOU MET ME. JUST SOME STUCK-UP BITCH UNTIL I MADE YOU INTERESTING! YOU'RE JUST SOME BASIC BITCH WHO BETTER WATCH HER BACK!,"* Zoe screaming to her classmate and friend Molly in the courtroom in Season 2 Episode 4

➢ woman-about-woman: *"Right now I have to go handle a bitch!,"* Annalise talking about the Assistant District Attorney Emily Sinclair in Season 2 Episode 6

- woman-referring to-herself: *"you're messing with the wrong bitch!,"* Annalise talking to Emily Sinclair in Season 2 Episode 7

- woman-to-woman: *"you're such a bitch!,"* Michaela speaking to Annalise in Season 3 Episode 1

- woman-about-man: *"you mean when his bitch ass ran away?,"* Annalise speaking to Laurel about Frank in Season 3 Episode 1

- woman-about-woman: *"Sam's sister. She was such a bitch.,"* Michaela says about Hannah Keating to her classmates, Connor, Laurel, Asher and Wes in Season 3 Episode 2

- woman-about-multiple people: *"I hate them! Every single one of their bitch ass lying faces.,"* Annalise says to Bonnie about her students, Connor, Laurel, Asher, Wes and Michaela in Season 3 Episode 2

- woman-to-group: *"Eighty grand in the bank bitch! What I say? Always bet black!,"* Michaela exclaiming happily to friends and other gamblers after winning in the casino, in Season 3 Episode 3

- woman-about-situation: *"Annalise got suspended for bitch-slapping a client. I'm not sure any of us should want to be here anymore.,"* Laurel says to Wes, Michaela, Asher and Connor in Season 3 Episode 4

- woman-to-man: *"Ain't jealousy a bitch?,"* Michaela says to classmate, Simon in Season 3 Episode 4

- woman-to-man: *"No the problem is you're a little bitch!,"* Annalise says to Nate in Season 3 Episode 4

- man-about-woman: *"Ding dong. The bitch is dead!,"* Simon says to the Keating five (Wes, Michaela, Laurel, Asher and Connor,) about Annalise's temporary suspension from Middleton University in Season 3 Episode 5

- man-to-woman: *"Your hillbilly came out when you were bitching-out Simon.,"* Asher says to Michaela referencing an earlier altercation she had with Simon in Season 3 Episode 5

- woman-to-group: *"Ooo! There goes my A bitches.,"* Michaela says to Laurel, Wes, Connor and Asher while preparing for a case in Season 3 Episode 7

- man-to-woman: *"You stupid bitch!,"* Nelson Duvall, one of Annalise's clients, says angrily to his sister, Karen, about her and her boyfriend's alleged involvement in an attempted poisoning case against their mother in Season 3 Episode 7

- woman-to-man: *"You want to change your life, or are you happy just to stay Annalise Keating's bitch?,"* Unnamed woman speaking to Frank persuasively to take bribe money in exchange for bugging Annalise's office in Season 3 Episode 8

- woman-speaking to-group: *Whoo! 96 bitches! Ha ha!,"* Michaela exclaims happily to her classmates after seeing her grade on an exam in Annalise's course in Season 3 Episode 9

- woman-to-man and man-to-woman: *"There he goes, signing up to be someone's bitch again.,"* Annalise says to Nate while arguing. *"You're the bitch!,"* Nate replies back furiously to Annalise in Season 3 Episode 9

- woman-to-woman: *"Bitch, will you just leave her be or do I need to drown you in your own piss?,"* Jasmine, Annalise's cellmate, says to the other cellmate, Claudia, while defending Annalise in Season 3 Episode 10

- woman-to-woman: *"You deaf, bitch?,"* Charmaine, a prisoner says to Annalise while they all shower in Season 3 Episode 11

- woman-about-woman: *"That bitch better not be in New York stalking the Mahoneys.,"* Michaela says to Asher about Laurel in Season 3 Episode 12

- woman- about-woman: *"This bitch.,"* Assistant District Attorney Rene Atwood says about Annalise in Season 3 Episode 13

- woman-to-man-about-woman: *"Do you have a problem? Because I understand why Laurel might be acting like a little bitch right now, but not you.,"* Bonnie says to Connor in Season 3 Episode 13

- woman-referring-to herself: *"Repulsive, disgusting, dried-up old bitch.,"* Woman #2 says in third person about herself in Season 3 Episode 14

- woman-about-woman: *"The bitch is spotless. We've been through every file we have on Atwood...twice.,"* Michaela speaking about Assistant District Attorney Rene Atwood to Annalise, Bonnie, Asher, Connor and Oliver in Season 3 Episode 14

- man-about-woman: *"I'm putting you in jail with that bitch!,"* District Attorney Denver says angrily to Nate about Annalise in Season 3 Episode 15

- woman-about-woman: *"No! I mean no more giving that bitch our time or energy.,"* Michaela speaking to Asher about Annalise in Season 4 Episode 1

- woman-to-woman: *"You one crazy ass bitch, I will give you that!,"* Jasmine, Annalise's client and former cellmate, speaking to her happily after Annalise tells Jasmine she is representing her pro bono in Season 4 Episode 2

- woman-about-woman: *"Hack this bitch!,"* Annalise says about Bonnie while loading a tape into a voice recorder in Season 4 Episode 4

- woman-referring to-herself: *"I hate most of the people in this firm. But I work with them cuz I'm a boss bitch and I'm trying to make you into one.,"* Tegan says to Michaela in Season 4 Episode 4

- woman-to-woman: *"Bitch we still hate you.,"* Claudia says to Annalise in Season 4 Episode 5

- woman-to-woman: *"Bitch please. I wanna see whose ass you beat next.,"* Claudia says to Annalise in 4 Episode 6

- woman-referring to-herself: *"The minute I take the stand they're going to ask me about everything--Wes, the fire, anything that makes me look like a crazy bitch.,"* Annalise speaking to Connor in Season 4 Episode 7

- woman-referring to-herself: "Antares is about to go public, the firm's gonna make millions and I can already smell the other partner's trying to take credit for something I made happen. I'll give a speech, shine in my own glory and let those man-children know this boss bitch don't play.," Tegan says about herself to Michaela in Season 4 Episode 7

- man-referring to-himself: *"I'm no one's bitch.,"* Asher says angrily to Michaela, Frank, Laurel and Oliver in Season 4 Episode 7

- woman-to-man: Simon to Michaela: *"What are you so worried about?"* Michaela to Simon: *"Excuse me?"* Simon to Michaela: *"You're doing that fake ass smile you plaster on when you're nervous."* Michaela: *"I don't do that."* Simon: *"Yeah you do. You do it when you get called on in class, you do it when you're taking exams,"* Michaela: *"or when I want to cut a bitch but can't 'cause I'm at a work function.,"* in Season 4 Episode 8

- woman-referring to-woman: *"Antares never could've expanded so quickly without our excellent international law department headed by fellow boss-bitch Aria Wilson.,"* Tegan giving her speech to her colleagues at the C&G law firm in Season 4 Episode 8

Scandal, another show produced, as well as created by Shonda Rhimes, features a scene in Season 4 Episode 6 where the character, President Fitzgerald Grant walks into the lead character, Olivia Pope's apartment and says, *"So, Abby's kind of a bitch."* Olivia immediately responds, *"Don't say that!" "The words used to describe women! If she was a man you'd say she was 'formidable' or 'bold' or 'right.'"* Yet, in Season 5 Episode 9, the scene consists of an exchange between the lead characters, Olivia Pope and the former First Lady, Mellie Grant where, in an attempt to encourage Mellie to persist through her prolonged and exhausting filibuster, Olivia says to her *"You're the biggest bitch I know!"*

Additionally, in Season 6, Episode 8, newcomer to the *Scandal* storyline is the political puppet master "mystery woman," played by actress Zoe Perry, who, in an exchange with Abby Wheland says, *"Oh Abby, I'm a real bitch, you just play one on tv."* In Season 7 Episode 5, the final season of the series, Olivia Pope says to Fitzgerald Grant while arguing, *"I see. So you think I've suddenly turned into some power hungry boss bitch who thinks she can play and use the President like a pawn?"* Finally, in Episode 7 of the final season, Olivia goes to speak with her "complex" mother, Maya Lewis, to ask for her aid in rescuing her pregnant friend Quinn Perkins who has been kidnapped by her even more duplicitous father, Eli Pope. Olivia responds to her mother's *"what am I getting out of it?"* question by saying, *"you can either be my mother or a bitch. What's it gonna be?"* Later in their conversation, Maya says, *"I'm talking about the fact that all your problems go away if this bitch dies."*

Writer, actress, comedian and producer Tina Fey has written and appeared in numerous well-known films and television shows and is largely known for her sitcom, *30 Rock*. Throughout the entire 7-season series, her character Liz/Elizabeth Lemon, the head writer and creator of a fictional sitcom on NBC, refers to herself as a "bitch" countless times, however, her character is a self-proclaimed feminist who's incredibly vocal about the empowerment of women, as well as the representation of women in media. Additionally, Tina Fey appears in the film *Sisters,* along with comedians Amy Poehler and Maya Rudolph, written by Paula Pell, which features the word "bitch" uttered 11 times solely by the female characters in the film. The successful and popular 2017 film, *Girl's Trip*, written by Tracy Oliver and Kenya Barris, featuring Queen Latifah, Jada Pinkett-Smith, Regina Hall and Tiffany Haddish, shows the four lead actresses calling themselves, each other and other women "bitches" a total of 14 times in the first 27 minutes and a sum total of 42 times throughout the entire two-hour film. It's important to mention that another gender-based slur used by the lead female characters towards other female characters in the film was "hoe," a colloquial term for "whore." Within four weeks after its premiere, *Girl's Trip* grossed over $100 million dollars domestically.

When I was a child growing up in the 90's, the word "bitch" was virtually absent from primetime television shows and essentially deemed a taboo. Coupled with the constant monitoring and sheltering my mother provided, it was essentially impossible for my sisters and I to see or hear the word at all. I do, however, recall hearing the term once while watching one of my favorite shows, *Living Single*. In Season 1 Episode 23, the leading ladies, Khadijah, Maxine, Regine and Synclaire playfully intrude their friends', Kyle and Overton's, poker game after being told it's a *"man's game."* After Khadijah wins the game against the men in attendance, Kyle's manager Lawrence stands up angrily and says, *"I did not come here to get whacked by these bitches."* All of the ladies and their friends, Kyle and Overton, stand up immediately and are irate at what Lawrence has called them. This scene was quite memorable for me, and I'm sure for many others, as it had a specific mission to illustrate the offensive and derogatory nature of this term, *not* to normalize it.

The question that surfaces to mind is, what factors have influenced such an astronomical rise in the frequent and widespread usage of the word "bitch" in television programs over the last 20 years? Many would strongly contend that, as more women have entered into behind-the-scenes roles as creators, executive producers and head writers, they have brought their feminist or womanist views into the space of media and thus, have "reappropriated" the term to use it freely as they see fit. In essence, the goal has been to withdraw the power of the word from their male counterparts. While there has been an increase in women's leadership roles (i.e. creators, writers, directors, executive producers, etc.) in television production, women actually only accounted for 26 percent of these roles between 2015-2016[6]. That translates into an overwhelming 84 percent of all the creative-leadership positions in existing television programming being controlled by men, most of whom are of White/European-American ancestry[7].

It all begins with the writing! The script or screenplay is the DNA or genetic code that animates the very life of a television program or film and if the writer possesses a patriarchal mindset (i.e. male writer) or an internalized sexist ethos (i.e. female writer,) then they will birth and propagate endless bloodlines of media that perpetuates antiquated narratives of women, which inevitably emerges into incessant television programming containing the "bitch narrative" like those referenced to earlier in this chapter.

The "Bitch" Narrative in Music

Some of the most influential musicians across genres have given rise to the pandemic that is the "culture of bitch" in music. Now, many would make an immediate leap to the trite, but accurate analysis of misogyny that has flourished in Rap and Hip-Hop music for over 30 years. However, critics often overlook or conveniently forget the raging sexism that prospered and fueled Rock music for more than 20 years between the 1970s and early 1990s. Globally renowned artists like, *Gun N Roses-"Used to Love Her," Aerosmith-"Bitches Brew," Metallica-"Ain't My Bitch," Rolling Stones-"Bitch," David Bowie-"Queen Bitch," Nazareth-"Hair of the Dog" and Elton John-"The Bitch is Back"* all normalized the usage of the word "bitch" in their music and thus, opened greater musical avenues for the term to be verbalized in songs.

In the 90's, our society witnessed an electric surge of the word "bitch" in the music industry, which was presented in an interesting bilateral dichotomy where, male musicians used the term primarily in a pejorative manner, while female artists used the word "bitch" largely as an "empowered title[1]." Male artists like *Dr. Dre, 2Pac, Nas, Ice Cube, Prodigy* and *Snoop Dogg* used the term religiously to express their views about women, evident in

---

[1] Many female artists also used "bitch" in a derogatory and demeaning manner towards other women, in addition to utilizing the word as a term of empowerment (i.e. bad bitch, queen bitch).

the 1992 song, *"Bitches Ain't Shit but Hoes and Tricks"* by Dr. Dre feat. Snoop Dogg with lyrics like *"Bitch can't hang with the streets, she found herself short, So now she's takin' me to court"* or the 1997 song with identical lyrics, *"Smack My Bitch Up,"* by the British beat group *Prodigy*. Alternatively, female artists like *Trina* and *Meredith Brooks* contributed to the era of "reappropriating" this term with lyrics like, *"Cause I'm the baddest bitch"* and *"I'm a bitch"* respectively.

Since the early 2000's leading to this present era, the reference "bad bitch" has all but become a criterion in music from both female and male artists in an attempt to "celebrate" or uphold women who project qualities of "independence," "strength" and "confidence," while simultaneously being portrayed in hypersexualized attire and accompanying poses and behaviors, exuding an unceasing sexual allure. More recently, the term "bad bitch" and usage of "bitch" in general has become widely used by many women in the music industry.

Globally renowned musicians *Rihanna, Nicki Minaj* and *Beyoncè* have been touted as some of the most influential female artists of the 21st century and have been upheld as representations of "feminism" in this new era. Lyrics from their most popular songs have included, *"But the hottest bitch in heels right here, No fear, and while you getting your cry on, I'm getting my fly on,"* from the song *"Hard,"* by *Rihanna*; *"And I ain't never liked a broke bitch, I ain't never fucked with your hoe, bitch,"* from the song *"Pose,"* by *Rihanna*; *"Bad bitches who I fuck with, mad bitches we don't fuck with,"* from the song *"Only,"* by *Nicki Minaj*; *"You know you that bitch when you cause all this conversation,"* from the song *"Formation,"* by *Beyoncè* and *"All of these bitches but he want the coldest yeah, cuz you prima donnas got nothin' on me; cuz Ima bad bitch, bad bitch,"* from the song *"Bad Bitch"* by *Beyoncè* and *Rihanna*.

In *Madonna's* 2015 music video for her song *"Bitch I'm Madonna,"* it features very young girls, approximately ages 8-12, singing along verbatim to *Madonna's* vocals saying , *"You're gonna love this, you can't touch this, 'cause I'm a bad bitch."* What then is the message, especially to young, impressionable and developing girls, to, on one hand, use the word "bitch" in a defamatory nature and then employ it as a term of empowerment about oneself and one's female friends?

Given the instant accessibility of music and videos due to incalculable instant streaming and downloading services, popular songs and their vacillating exploitations on the term "bitch," like the aforementioned ones and countless others, flourish. With $54.6 million in digital music revenue in the United States accounting for $42.93 billion in total revenue for the music industry, this capitalist "culture of bitch" furthers the message that women are "bitches" and *this* is the norm[8].

The "Bitch" Narrative in Books, Clothing and Alcohol

Other media or advertising sources that have undeniably contributed to the "culture of bitch" include books, apparel, food and alcoholic beverages. Books, such as *"How to Be A Bad Bitch"* by *Amber Rose,* *"Why Men Love Bitches"* by *Sherry Argov,* *"Skinny Bitch"* by *Rory Freedman and Kim Barnouin,* and *"The Bitch Switch"* by *Omarosa Manigualt* have capitalized exorbitantly from their exploitation of the word "bitch" as a tactic to provoke women to either: a) embrace their "inner bitch" or b) adopt "bitch-like" qualities to achieve the desired power, success and independence in their careers, as well as employ their nonstop sexual siren-like appeal to men.

Apparel companies, such as *Caviar Blaque Apparel* and *One Bad Bitch*, have created entire ventures built on tenets analogous to those purported in the aforementioned books, featuring beguiling slogans like *"Bad Bitches Link Up"* and *"Quality Stitches for Quality Bitches"* on women's shirts, dresses and other clothing.

Alcohol, wine and liquor distributors like *Sweet Bitch, Ivana Bitch, Raging Bitch Ale, Skinny Bitch* and many others have also contributed largely to and profited from the capitalist normalization of "bitch."

The "culture of bitch" is undeniably entrenched in our societal DNA and is manifested in every limb that is a part of this body that is our world. Where does this ethos of women being "bitches" derive from and moreover, who or what is directly responsible for its existence? Are we as individuals liable for the perpetuation of this term or are larger institutions?

CHAPTER 2

PIERCING THE SHELL:

Bitch: The Chicken or The Egg Phenomenon

As demonstrated in Chapter 1, every single one of us is affected, influenced and touched by the "culture of bitch." We, unfortunately, reside in a society saturated with this term through numerous mediums that support and directly profit from its very existence and it is these sources that perpetuate the life force of the "culture of bitch," which are unequivocally fixed into our daily experiences and mental recordings. Therefore, it can be quite difficult to locate a single source liable for its creation, existence and continuation. Frequently, the blame for the "culture of bitch" is cast onto the elusive, never fully defined entity, "society" as in, *"it's 'society's' fault that we're in this place"* or *"'society' is the reason why sexism exists."* But ask yourself, what is a society exactly and what is it comprised of? Every civilization, including our own in the United States, has been established and is upheld by two very integral forces: people and established structures or as I will refer to in this book, *micro* and *macro systems*.

The relationship between people and established structures is mutually linked and thus, one cannot survive without the other. People possess the beliefs and ideas (*micro system*) that are consequently infused into established structures (*macro systems.*) For example, a woman calls her girlfriends "bitches" because she grew up seeing her mother or an influential female relative modeling this behavior. Those beliefs and ideologies about the women's identities are then carried over into her career in writing or literary publishing, clothing design, film production, music or scripted television. Regarding the "culture of bitch," both people (i.e. *micro systems*) *and* established structures (i.e. *macro systems*) are therefore responsible for the perpetuation of this phenomenon.

Macro Systems

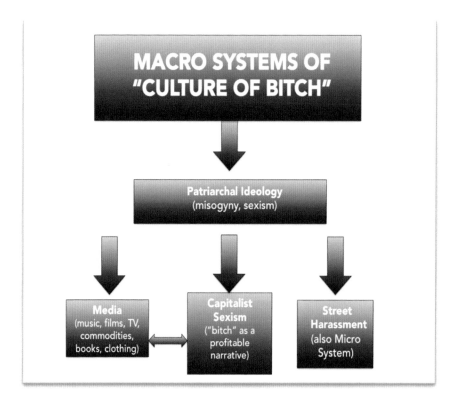

Source: J.R. Baker-Flowers

The *macro systems* that have given rise to and fuel the "culture of bitch" are: a) Patriarchal Ideologies, b) Media, c) Capitalist Sexism and d) Street Harassment.

Patriarchal Ideologies

Patriarchal ideologies are the systematized set of thoughts and beliefs that men are inherently superior to and more powerful than women and should therefore, have dominion over women entirely. Ideas rooted in patriarchy can be thought of as the blueprint from which sexism, misogynistic actions and the overall social and institutional oppression of women extend from. But where does this ethos [patriarchy] derive and originate from?

Vivian C. Fox found that Judeo-Christian religious ideology was one of the most influential factors that heavily influenced Western society's views of and treatment towards women, as well as established a "hierarchy of gender." Regarding religion's influence on the formation and continuation of patriarchal ideology, Fox contends that,

> One of the earliest and most significant of the patriarchal systems was the Hebrews, despite their continued polytheistic worship and their acceptance of female Goddesses. For the Hebrews created a theology, passed on in western tradition, which proclaimed God to be alone, "eternal, omnipotent, omnipresent, omniscient, just, good, compassionate, merciful and benevolent" and masculine as his two names, Yahweh and Elohim were revealed to all HIS children[9].

Fox further posits that "the rib version" of the Judeo-Christian creation story has heavily reinforced the notion of the innate subordinate role of women. The first introduction to a woman and the nature of womanhood within the Judeo-Christian text is Eve, "the temptress," who seduced Adam into eating the forbidden fruit after falling prey to the evil serpent. As Judeo-Christianity flourished resulting from global colonialism, along with it came the sweeping philosophy regarding the inferiority and "weakness" of women who must be properly led by men entirely or their husbands; this deeply rooted ethos has and continues to permeate sociocultural, political and economic institutions all over the world.

Examining the religious influence on the construct of marriage, it's very evident these patriarchal philosophies have greatly influenced the hierarchical dynamic between husbands and wives:

> *"Wives, submit yourselves to your own husbands as you do to the Lord;" "For the husband is the head of the wife as Christ is the head of the church, his body, of which he is the Savior;" "Now as the church submits to Christ, so also wives should submit to their husbands in everything,"*[10].

Additionally, the propagation of marital chastisement or punishment towards women was considered the duty of the husband in exercising his "natural," "God-given" power over his wife. Eve's punishment from God for her sin was that she obey her husband "*a dictum joined by the common law's sanction that husbands rule their household and impose 'moderate correction' when necessary.*[11]"

Expounding on this, Judeo-Christian patriarchy is so normalized in our society that phrases, such as *"rule of thumb,"* are routinely used and integrated regularly in conversation as a result of the multigenerational unconscious acceptance of misogyny. This phrase, *"rule of thumb,"* was shaped both by William Tyndale's pamphlet, *Obedience of a Christian Man,* (i.e. *"let the woman therefore fear her husband...that she obey him*) and 16th, 17th and 18th century British and American laws permitting husbands to physically chastise their wives "as long as the punitive stick was no thicker than his thumb"[12].

Ideas, ideologies and beliefs are the foundation upon which behaviors, language, actions, systematized policies, socially sanctioned mores and entire institutions are erected! It is glaringly obvious and quite undeniable that patriarchy *is* the foundation that has built the "culture of bitch" and encourages the very existence of this word.

Media

As highlighted in Chapter 1, Media is another highly influential *macro system* contributing to the "culture of bitch," given its global reach, trillion dollar revenue infrastructure and multi-sensory impact.[2] The age-old question, "*does art imitate life or does life imitate art?*," merely probes the symbiotic relationship between music, films, television, books and fashion and the complexities of the human experience. While there is an irrefutable mutual connection between artistic expression and life, the collective economic agency and sociopolitical influence of media as an institution is astounding.

Stop for a moment and think about how your life, your daily experiences, purchasing habits, food cravings, hobbies, career interests and even your friendships and intimate partner relationships are influenced by media:

> ♦ You watch a new music video from your favorite artist and see an amazing pair of shoes they're wearing and you think, "I would LOVE to have those shoes! Where can I buy those?!"

---

[2] Multi-sensory impact, meaning stimulating one's visual, auditory, emotional, touch or tactile senses and taste.

> ♦ *When your eyes gaze upon a massive billboard while driving to work, displaying an enticing, mouthwatering plate of food, you think, "I can't WAIT to eat lunch! Where am I gonna eat today?"*
>
> ♦ *When you're on Facebook, YouTube or Instagram and view a video of your favorite or a highly popular social media personality doing a tutorial on makeup looks, a tutorial on wigs and other hairstyles, OOTD (outfit of the day) fashion looks or discussing their health and fitness regimen, you instantly think, "Girl YASSSS! Where can I get that makeup?!" or, "YAASSS HONEY! Where can I buy that wig or those hair products?!" or, "SLAY GIRL SLAY!! Let me find out I can order these clothes online!" or "Yes ma'am! Let me get my life and start making these green smoothies and drinking this FitTea!."*
>
> ♦ *While watching your favorite television program or favorite movie and see a scene with the "perfect" date that leads to the "perfect" relationship and potentially an "idyllic" marriage, your mind is filled with thoughts like, "When will I meet someone like 'this?'," or "Awwwww! I want a relationship/man/woman like 'that!'"*

Isn't it fascinating to visualize this portrait of our lives and to reflect on what we consider as the most routine, basic and personal decisions we make are *actually* guided and largely controlled by dominant media sources? Media *is* art and thus, it engages our rudimentary senses while simultaneously absorbing the message(s) it promotes.

As your eyes gaze upon a billboard, t-shirt or fashion accessory, a magazine cover or photograph containing the word "bitch," your eyes instantaneously transport that message and content to your brain where it is housed, stored and awaits to be recalled and used later. As your ear buds filter your favorite songs from your phone, and as your ears catch the waves of the music pulsating over the radio, the catchy tune with beats echoing the word "bitch" seeps into your ears and vibrates throughout your cerebellum, hippocampus, thalamus and amygdala, activating your mind's cognition, memory formation, movement, mood and emotional responses[13].

I raised the question before and will ask it again now: what is the best way to disseminate a message, campaign or viewpoint? MEDIA! Remember, we reside in a society built on patriarchy and despite its antiquated origins, the progenitor patriarchy and its offspring, sexism, misogyny and chauvinism *are* the fabric upon which anti-womanist behaviors and sociopolitical female oppression is woven into our society. This includes media. Media surrounds us in every manner and the decisions we make or *think* we make autonomously are highly informed and moreover, controlled by their influence.

Capitalist Sexism

Capitalist Sexism, a segment of media, is an additional *macro system* breeding and furthering the "culture of bitch." Capitalism is usually defined as an economic system characterized by 1) private or corporate owners who control capital goods, 2) investments determined by private decision, and 3) prices, production, and the distribution of goods that are determined mainly by competition in a free market[14]. Sexism is defined as 1) prejudice or discrimination based on one's sex, especially discrimination towards women and 2) behaviors and attitudes that foster stereotypes of social roles based on sex[15].

With our society's history rooted in a patriarchal state, it goes without saying that the blueprint of capitalism parallels to the structure of sexism in that it "is a system that compounds and exacerbates inequality. It is, simply put, a system that requires inequality for it to thrive and function effectively"[16].

In alignment with Media, Capitalist Sexism is underscored by large multinational media corporations, such as ABC, Time Warner, CBS and News Corporation, unfailingly financially backing or "green-lighting" the production of a multitude of sexist or gender-biased media, like *The Real Housewives* leviathan or scripted television programs whose primary content consists of the word "bitch"[17]. The more these billion dollar global corporations unceasingly pour dollars into sexist media, the demand for the "bitch" narrative rises, urging and coaxing more writers, showrunners and producers to create films, television programs and even advertisements that center on the usage of this inherently derogatory term.

Refer for a moment back to Chapter 1 and the list of television shows and their respective scripts containing the word "bitch." The multinational media corporations that house, own and support the very production of these shows include those mentioned above, yet *they* are owned by the parent companies, Comcast, The Walt Disney Company and Viacom. Comcast or Comcast Corporation, the largest media company in the world with an annual revenue of $74.51 billion owns NBC, Oxygen and Bravo to name a few. If you recall, *The Real Housewives* genus and it's accompanying spinoff shows are featured on Bravo, which again, is owned by Comcast. Another television program housed under this conglomerate, that is equally saturated with the term "bitch" is, *The Bad Girls Club,* featured on Oxygen, a channel whose programming, viewed in over 65 percent of American households[18], is specifically designed to target women, especially younger women, ages 18-34[19].

The Walt Disney Company owns the popular television channels ABC and Lifetime and some of the most popular and highly syndicated programs featured on these stations include, *Scandal, How to Get Away With Murder, Little Women: LA, Little Women: Atlanta* and *Bring It.* Every single one of these shows, both scripted and reality-based, are laden with "bitch" as a "series regular." Finally, Viacom is an American media conglomerate that owns both cable television and film companies. These include, MTV, VH1, Paramount Pictures, BET and others, which all largely contain music videos, television programming and movies that capitalize from characters, storylines and music with the "bitch" narrative. And what's more alarming is the reality that, the deeper consumers and viewers fall under the spell of these slanted shows, the ratings continue to rise, which in turn increases the very revenue the multinational media corporations use to create and produce the aforementioned programs, and more, with the "bitch" plot.

Consider this: when people say *"sex sells,"* what they *really* mean is the sexual objectification of women sells. Cocaine, crack, heroin, meth, fast food and alcohol sell too and yet, people are tormented by and die from the destructive influences of these institutionalized maladies every single day! Capitalist Sexism is no different. It fuels the media-based economic, creative and tactically targeted oppression of women, where their very identities and stories are commodified, dehumanized and reduced to well-timed punch lines and catchy, pithy slogans heard and absorbed by billions of people all around the world!

Street Harassment

Street Harassment is another *macro system* that supports the "culture of bitch" in our society. Every woman, at some point in her life, has experienced or will experience a form of Street Harassment. Catcalls, leering, honking, unwarranted physical groping and sexual gestures in public spaces, usually by males towards their female counterparts, are all forms of gender-based Street Harassment. In many cases, after a woman either outwardly rejects the unwarranted advances of harassers or ignores the assailant and walks away, she is called a *"bitch,"* which serves as tool for gender-based violence or assault.

While the actions of Street Harassment derive from an individual's behavior (i.e. catcalling, groping, etc.,) this is a *macro system*, (i.e. an institution,) given that within our legislative and judicial system, there are very few or no laws specifically designed to address it. Furthermore, for the broad laws available to victims of Street Harassment, they are 1) not widely publicized to inform citizens of their rights and 2) the process of convicting those culpable is unregulated and not widely broadcast.

"Assault and/or battery laws are not relevant to Street Harassment in every state, but when they are, you will find them listed under the 'Verbal Harassment' or 'Groping' sections of those states"[20]. Catcalling and unwarranted sexually explicit language or verbal harassment are deemed as acts of assault, whereas nonconsensual physical contact, like groping, is considered battery. In California, sexual battery, (i.e. touching a non-consenting person's intimate body parts for the purpose of sexual arousal, sexual gratification and/or sexual abuse,) under Title 8, Chap. 9 §234.4(e), the assailant can be found guilty and penalized with a misdemeanor, which is found punishable with a $2,000 fine and/or up to 6 months in jail. In Washington, D.C., Misdemeanor Sexual Abuse & Second Degree Sexual Abuse under Title 22, Subtitle I, Chap. 30 §3006, it is illegal for anyone to have sexual contact with someone if s/he should have known that the sexual contact was without consent. Sexual contact is defined as touching, either under or over clothing, another person's genitals, groin, inner thigh, butt, or breast with the intent to: a) Humiliate, b) Degrade, c) Harass or d) Arouse or gratify sexual desire. If a street harasser is charged and found guilty, the penalty is categorized as a misdemeanor sexual abuse punishable by a fine of up to $1,000 and/or 180 days in jail.

Although victims of Street Harassment are able to report these crimes and even file charges, navigating the judicial system can be quite a dizzying and opaque journey, due to the generalization of these laws. Moreover, embedded within the structure of these laws lies an inherent gender inequity. Again, given that our society was built and still operates on a culture of intrinsic patriarchy, "the laws in the United States have historically been written by white, straight men, and often are written and enforced to only protect against the types of violence, harassment, and intrusion that they experience" ([21].) Take for example the First Amendment. This amendment to the Constitution grants U.S. citizens the right to "freedom of speech," thus aggressors generally feel protected and even just in their verbal assaults because "offensive language," like *"hey sexy!"* or *"bitch,"* are not considered intimidating speech, which the First Amendment regulates, [or at least claims to regulate.]

As lawmakers throughout history have categorically been White men, they've seldom faced gender-based Street Harassment[3] and therefore, have never experienced the daily fear, anxiety, anger and lack of safety millions of women have felt and feel regularly in public spaces.

Lastly, because our society has operated on a fundamental patriarchal framework for thousands of years, this anti-womanist ideology has given rise to structural campaigns that espouse and perpetuate victim blaming and victim responsibility. The Sussex Police force marketed a campaign in April 2015, with the message, *"Which one of your mates is the most vulnerable on a night out? The one you leave behind." "Many sexual assaults could be prevented."* This campaign enforces the notion that women should not leave their friends alone or let them go away with strangers as a way to "prevent getting raped"[22]. The Pittsburgh Action Against Rape developed a rape prevention campaign for college students to highlight the connection between alcoholic

---
[3] This excludes homosexual and LGBTQIA identified White men who experience ongoing street harassment and hate crimes regularly.

intoxication and rape[23]. To drive the organization's campaign forward, one of the visuals used consists of the outline of a woman's lower torso in the shape of a martini glass mimicking a vagina as the focal point, with the words, *"On college campuses, 75% of rape survivors reported being intoxicated at the time of the attack."* Despite the organization's intention and efforts to both drive awareness regarding rape on college campuses and the protection of potential victims, the message that women are responsible for any form of assault they directly experience screams volumes! While rape is considered more severe and thus, illegal and prosecutable than Street Harassment, it is imperative to understand and acknowledge that rape is [usually] a gradual or escalating predatory behavior and commonly begins with sexualized verbal attacks that lead to groping and then results in acts of rape and other forms of sexual assault.

These *macro systems*, Patriarchal Ideologies, Media, Capitalist Sexism and Street Harassment, have designed the genetic framework for the body that is the "culture of bitch." These collective entities have yielded a surreptitiously normalized operating system, where the social, cultural, political and media-based oppression and maltreatment of women is not only customary and monetarily rewarded, it has also silenced and reduced women's identities and narratives to diminutive, depersonalized objects.

Micro Systems

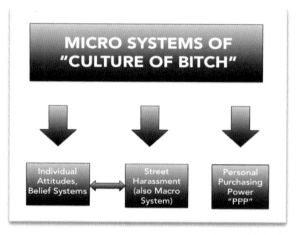

Source: J.R. Baker-Flowers

Since large institutions, or *macro systems,* are incapable of existing solitarily, it's necessary to acknowledge the role of people or *micro systems* that have also influenced the "culture of bitch." These *micro systems* include, a) Individual Attitudes and Belief Systems, b) Street Harassment and c) Personal Purchasing Power (PPP©.)

Individual Attitudes and Belief Systems

One of the commonalities of the human experience, which unites people across racial/ethnic, sex, gender, sexual orientation, socio-economic, religious and other cultural backgrounds, is how we form or develop our attitudes and belief systems. Attitudes can be described as a learned or adopted evaluation of viewing people, cultures, objects and social issues. This is usually the result of direct personal experience(s) or upbringing and these acquired evaluations or attitudes can have a profound influence on behavior[21]. I will use myself as an example on the formation of attitudes and how that creates belief systems and in turn, influences behavior:

> *As you can probably tell by now, my attitude about the word "bitch" is that it's a deplorable slur rooted in antiquated sexism. I possess this stance or belief system because 1) I never saw or heard my mother speak to or about her friends this way, nor did she refer to another woman in this manner, 2) my mother always espoused principles of sisterhood and feminine unity and 3) taught me that the word is dehumanizing.*
>
> *Additionally, I've always had an innate passion for women's rights, racial justice, lgbtq rights and social change in general, which was cultivated during my graduate education at Clark University. I have also had numerous personal experiences being called a "bitch," almost always when I've defended myself after an occurrence of verbal and physical Street Harassment (i.e. male groping) and have also been called a "bitch" for being "too outspoken" about varying issues of equality.*

> *Due to my collective experiences, my belief system is that no one should use the term under any circumstances because it perpetuates demeaning and misogynistic stereotypes of women. This has influenced my behavior to speak out on the "culture of bitch" by directing and producing a documentary and multimedia initiative on this issue, as well as authoring this book to awaken and inform others on this critical sociopolitical matter and inspire sustainable transformation.*

Typically, many people oversimplify their personal attitudes or belief systems as *"just how I am,"* but given our complexities as human beings, we are never *"just"* anything!

From the moment we enter into the world, our psyches, consciousness and neurological circuitry are shaped by impressions and messages from a variety of elements around us. These elements are the most influential constituents in our lives and include: a) immediate familial ties, b) neighborhood, community and social connections, c) religious affiliations, d) culture and e) media. For the purpose of this book, I will narrow my focus to immediate familial relationships and media. I know, I know! You're thinking, *"Media AGAIN?!"* Trust me, before you finish reading this book, you'll understand why media is such a frequently recurring and vital theme.

Our immediate familial ties have profound impacts on our attitude formation. The experiences, messages and teachings we acquire, largely during our formative years, from parents/guardians, grandparents, aunts and uncles leave lasting impressions on the attitudes, perspectives and beliefs we hold. Take a moment to think about how influential the interactions, teachings and conversations from your immediate familial ties have been on your attitudes and beliefs regarding women.

What are your fundamental beliefs about women's "roles" in society, women's bodies, women's identities, women's sexuality, etc.? Now ask yourself, a) *why* do you have these beliefs?, b)*when* did you first begin to develop your belief system? and c)*who* was the person or persons that guided these attitudes?

Chances are you recalled significant past experiences engaging with your immediate family members, perhaps during your childhood, while tracing your attitudes and beliefs back to their origins.

Let's examine some common scenarios countless people have experienced regarding the impact their immediate familial ties have had in shaping their views, belief systems and behaviors about and towards women in relation to the word "bitch":

⇒ A young male child playing in the living room, overhears his parents arguing close by in the kitchen. He hears his father say to his mother, *"sometimes you can be a real bitch you know that?!"*

⇒ A mother, shopping in a department store with her two daughters, gets into a slightly heated exchange with the female sales clerk. When the argument subsides, the mother turns away from the checkout line with her daughters in tow and utters, *"BITCH!,"* under her breath.

⇒ A mother and her sister are watching *The Real Housewives of Atlanta*, drinking wine and conversing about what's happening on the show. They laugh and joke about the show's characters and make remarks like, *"Yaaaasss bitch! Tell that bitch how it is!"* Their children are playing together in front of them.

⇒ A father is talking with two guy friends about dating, women and relationships in the den. His young teenage son enters the room to ask his father a question and he hears one of the men say, *"yeah man, you have to watch out for these gold diggin' bitches nowadays!"* His father looks at him and says, *"You hear that boy? Don't trust these women out here."*

⇒ A young girl, age 12, is being scolded by her mother for not washing the dishes from the previous night. Her mother yells, *"How many times have I told you to wash the dishes?!"* The girl responds, *"I know mom geez!"* Her mother replies, *"don't speak to me that way. Just do the dishes!"* The girl huffs and says, *"uuugghhh! Fine, I'll wash them!"* Her mom says, *"ok, you're acting like a little bitch!"*

While these scenarios may not mirror your personal experiences, they *are* the realities of an incalculable number of people in our society, some of which you may even know.

The immediate familial structure (i.e. parents/guardians, grandparents, etc.,) serves as the initial and foundational model or teacher for social interactions and communication. It is also the nucleus for disseminating ideology, cultural identity and expectations of gender roles. Thus, for someone who has grown-up in an immediate familial structure where calling a woman or girl a "bitch" was and/or is the norm, it is probable that both their attitudes about and behavior towards women will emulate their early experiences[4]. Therefore, it's vital to acknowledge that our early interactions with our immediate familial ties are greatly influential in the development of our attitudes and belief systems.

Media is another prominent constituent in the formation of one's attitudes and belief system. As discussed in Chapter 1 and earlier

---

[4] It's important to note that, although someone may grow-up in a household where the word "bitch" is said frequently, this does not determine their destiny, nor guarantee they will adopt the same behaviors. However, there is a high probability that their early introduction to this term may impact their attitudes about and behaviors towards women.

in Chapter 2 of this book, we reside in a society that is highly inundated with and controlled by numerous media sources. Moreover, due to the immediate accessibility we have to media, (i.e. ownership of multiple mobile devices, instant media streaming sources, ebooks, etc.,) our multi-sensory connection to media-based content with the word "bitch" is irrefutably high.

Additionally, with the astronomical rates of media consumption and consumerism within this society (see Chapter 1,) it's undeniable that our perspectives and attitudes about women are largely informed and shaped by the media we routinely engage with. "The use of the word 'bitch' tripled in the last decade alone," growing from 431 uses on a total of 103 prime-time programs in 1998 to 1,277 uses on 685 prime-time television shows in 2007[25]. What's more jarring is that, under the Federal Communication Commission (FCC,) the word "bitch" does not fall under their obscene, profane and indecent language guidelines, whereas the words "fuck" and "shit" do[26]. And with the incessant negative portrayals of women in visual media that reinforce patriarchal and oppressive stereotypes, it's quite easy to draw the connection between media's influence on an individual's attitudes and belief system about women.

Far too often, "successful women have been portrayed in pop culture as cold and heartless — 'a bitch'"[27]. Other portrayals of women in media that elicit the "bitch" response are:

- ❖ women who are highly intelligent, quiet, nerdy and unsociable
- ❖ women who are sex positive (i.e. having or promoting an open or progressive attitude towards sex and sexuality)
- ❖ women who outwardly "challenge" male counterparts and don't remain "in their place"
- ❖ women who are physically fit, thin or small-framed
- ❖ women who wear form fitting, "provocative" clothing
- ❖ women who speak their minds and are direct

❖ women who are materialistic

Given that 99 percent of households own an average of two television sets, the average North American spends over 5.11 hours per day watching television and the average child watches 1,480 minutes or 24.66667 hours per week of television[28], coupled with the fact that the word "bitch" has more than tripled in its appearance on prime-time shows since the late 1990's, it's clear that the, "woman=bitch" media storyline is not only prolific, it informs the attitudes, perspectives and beliefs of its viewers, while also influencing their behaviors. Furthermore, as Columnist Theresa Schneider contends,

> The so-called standards of indecent language protect children from poop but allow impressionable listeners and viewers to learn that calling a woman a bitch is not only socially acceptable, but normal and sometimes funny. Essentially, by allowing "bitch" and not "s---", the FCC exposes children to the idea that it is OK to degrade women[29].

In addition to television as a major conduit to molding beliefs and attitudes about women, music and music videos, social media, books, clothing, photographs and commodities containing the word "bitch" also greatly influence our society's perspectives about and interactions with women. Numerous online stores create, sell and distribute apparel with the message *"bad bitch,"* which suggests that only a certain type of woman, usually scantily clad or completely naked, is deemed "desirable," "strong," and "on top" due to her "sexually provocative" nature. Compounded by the incalculable number of music videos, songs, memes, literature, alcohol, food, beverages and GIFs that contain and use the word "bitch," in both "reappropriated" and pejorative ways, the message that woman is synonymous with "bitch" is circulated on a non-stop media cycle permeating every single one of our senses. The more we consume, ingest, and engage with this material, our minds, attitudes, consciousness, neurological responses and ultimate behaviors are primed and fixed to view and treat women as "bitches" *and* sexualized objects.

Our Individual Attitudes and Belief Systems are without a doubt, the most powerful, basic and fundamental codes that guide how we operate and see the world, as they literally create our daily realities, behaviors and interactions with the entire world, including the people around us, as well as with ourselves. Understanding *why* we have certain attitudes and beliefs can help us to better recognize issues, like the "culture of bitch" and how *we* contribute to it.

Street Harassment

Street Harassment, an extension of Individual Attitudes and Belief Systems, is another *micro system* contributing to the "culture of bitch." Again, Street Harassment consists of behaviors such as catcalls, leering, honking, unwarranted physical groping and sexual gestures in public spaces. This contributes to the "culture of bitch," in that, when a woman doesn't "comply" with these behaviors from her assailant and either speaks out against it or physically fights back, she is without question called a *"bitch."* While these actions aren't gender specific, the data explicitly highlights that more women are the victims of Street Harassment from their male counterparts[30]. What causes male street harassers to behave in the aforementioned ways?

Earlier in this chapter, we discussed Patriarchal Ideologies as the institutionalized set of thoughts and beliefs that, men are inherently superior to and more powerful than women; ideas rooted in patriarchy are the blueprint from which sexism and misogynistic actions and behaviors derive from. As a result, women are verbally harassed, groped, catcalled, winked and honked at in public spaces due to patriarchal attitudes and a belief system of the harasser that 1) men are inherently superior to women, 2) men have basic sexual urges and 3) women are isolated sexual body parts, created solely for their male gaze and for their personal sexual gratification. These attitudes are directly shaped and influenced by men's experiences with Immediate Familial Ties and Media⁵.

Let's review some common scenarios many males have experienced regarding the impact their immediate familial ties have had in shaping their attitudes, belief systems and behaviors towards women and their roles in Street Harassment:

- a young boy is playing outside in the front yard directly in front of his father, uncles and father's friends from work. All of the men begin shouting, *"Damn look at that ass!! Aye girl...damn you fine!,"* to a woman walking by down the street. She turns to the men and says, *"Ugh, shut up!"* The men laugh and one of the boy's uncles says, *"haha, that bitch is trippin'!"*

- a teenage male is sitting in the living room watching a sports game with his father and a commercial comes on. The father changes the station to a music video channel and a woman wearing a string bikini thong saunters across the screen as the lyrics, *"you say you want a bad bitch, baby now you have it"* from BeBe Rexha's *"Bad Bitch,"* serve as the soundtrack to her movements. The father's eyes, fixed on the image of the woman, utters under his breath, *"Look at that ass and those titties! God damn!"* The father sees his son looking at him, smirks, and the father says, *"she was sexy huh?!"*

- two young boys, brothers, are playing on the stoop of their apartment building. Their grandfather is sitting in a lawn chair among his friends and son. Three ladies with shopping bags walk by and their grandfather says, *"Lord have*

---

[5] These attitudes are also shaped from vicarious learning experiences with communal ties and neighborhood culture, (i.e. a male child grows up witnessing a culture of Street Harassment in their neighborhood where groups of older teenage boys and men catcall, grope and sexually harass teenage girls and women.)

mercy...do you see the ass on that one in the red?" Some of the other men reply, *"Oh, YEAH! And her front ain't too bad either! I sure would like to get my hands on those!"* One of the women overhears the comments and confronts the group of men for their statements and says, *"y'all ought to be ashamed of yourselves! You can't talk to us that way at all! And how can you speak that way in front of these children?!"* The young boys stop playing and look at the exchange happening between the women and the group of men. The grandfather says loudly, *"Listen bitch! Don't bring my grandkids into this. Take your ass on somewhere!"* The other men giggle and make additional lewd comments as the women turn and walk away.

While not all men have experienced these occurrences during their formative years from Immediate Familial Ties, many of you reading this certainly know of male colleagues, friends, family members or associates who have. As a direct result, they have probably behaved in a manner that qualifies as Street Harassment and subsequently called a woman a "bitch" after she defended herself and failed to "submit" to his misogynistic advances.

So you see, it is the [patriarchal] attitudes and [sexist] belief systems that give rise to the behaviors that typify Street Harassment, which has become a societal infrastructure (i.e. *macro system*) not wholly regulated by the judicial system.

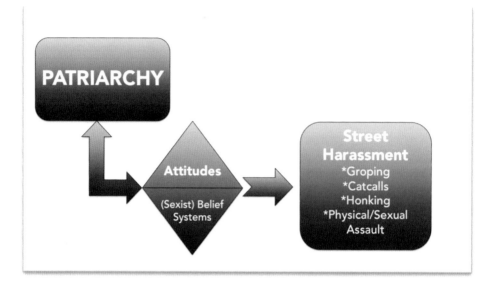

Source: J.R. Baker-Flowers

This diagram highlights the correlation between Patriarchy, the formation of sexist attitudes and belief systems and resulting sexist behaviors, like Street Harassment.

Personal Purchasing Power (PPP©)

Finally, another *micro system* that directly contributes to the continuation of the "culture of bitch" is Personal Purchasing Power (PPP©.) We've all been there. Counting down the days until payday so we can rush out and buy that "new phone," "new dress or new outfit," "new makeup palette," "new shoes," "new album," or that "new book." It's like the money is, as my mother would always say when I was a child, "burning a hole in your pocket" and you just *have* to spend it! Well, it's this insatiable desire to spend your money as quickly as you get it that clothing designers and retailers, electronic manufacturers, food and beverage companies and countless other *macro systems* are literally banking on.

The reason for this, apart from the ultimate goal of making money is, your spending patterns via your hard earned dollars informs them: a) if you like/love the good or service they're manufacturing and producing and b) if they should continue creating that good or service; basic Supply and Demand.

In this [U.S.] westernized, capitalist-driven, material-centric society, voracious consumerism has become a normalized, fundamental way of life. And due to the advent and meteoric rise of the internet, which birthed social networking and social media, the ethos of instant gratification, celebrity idolization and self-indulgence "on-tap" is kith and kin to "the American Dream"[6;31].

Moreover, with Media's constant multi-sensory presence and influence on our life's basic decisions, the desire to "buy, buy, buy" and "spend, spend, spend," seems to rest at the forefront of our minds. With regards to the "culture of bitch," how you use your Personal Purchasing Power (PPP©) informs and advises companies, such as record labels, retail stores, literary publishing houses and multimedia conglomerates that you want them to continue creating, manufacturing and distributing goods and services that capitalize off of the word and narrative of "bitch."

If you recall from Chapter 1, we reviewed the diverse areas of media consumption related to the statistics on digital music download revenue totals, social media engagement, television viewership and mobile electronic ownership. Looking deeper into these areas, the relationship between consumer's dollars and the "culture of bitch" becomes more discernible:

❖ *"How to Be a Bad Bitch,"* by Amber Rose published by Simon & Schuster reached #2 in the iTunes audiobook store in 2016[32]

---

[6] It is important to acknowledge that North American Westernized capitalist ideology, cultural practices and lifestyle has become adopted by other countries and cultures worldwide due to systemic globalization. Consequently, Westernized capitalist political and economic values are now a global ideological framework.

- Rihanna's, "*Bitch Better Have My Money*" record sold 108,000 copies in the first four days of its release; the following week, the record sold an additional 133,000 copies; it also sold 43,000 digital downloads and was streamed 10 million times in the United States by July 2015[33]. Recording Industry Association of America (RIAA) certified the song double platinum on July 25, 2015 reporting over 2,000,000 digital copies[34]

- Sherry Argov, author of "*Why Men Love Bitches,*" "*Why Men Marry Bitches*" and "*Why Men Love Bitches Uncensored*" has been ranked #1 internationally, voted one of the "Ten Most Iconic Relationship Books," New York Times Bestseller and Los Angeles Times Bestseller. Her books have been translated into over 30 languages[35]

- "*Flawless,*" by Beyoncè, featuring the famous lyrics "*bow down bitches,*" had 1,300,000 sales worldwide with over 900,000 digital sales within the United States[36] and over 49,217,804 video streaming views on YouTube

- "*The Pink Print*" album by Nicki Minaj sold over 2,661,000 copies worldwide, featuring the songs, "*Buy A Heart,* "*Want Some More,*" "*Favorite*" and the others below, each containing the word "bitch"[37]
   a. "*Only*" with 183,000 in digital sales
   b. "*Anaconda*" with 850,000 in digital sales

- Rory Freedman and Kim Barnouin, authors of *The Skinny Bitch Diet,* has sold over 1.1 million copies[38]

Personal Purchasing Power (PPP©) is not only isolated to your financial impact as a consumer, but it also pertains to how you purchase goods and services with your time and energy in the form of viewership and sharing web-based content. For example:

- ❖ *"Bitch Better Have My Money"* record by Rihanna, exceeded 100 million views on YouTube in November 2016, making it the 1st ever age-restricted VEVO certified video[39]

- ❖ *"The Real Housewives of Atlanta"* doubled the ratings of the other *Real Housewives* franchises and on March 1, 2015, drew 3.737 million live viewers for that single episode[40]

- ❖ ABC's *How to Get Away With Murder* had 4.8 million viewers overall, ages 18-49 per episode in 2016[41]

- ❖ *American Horror Story: Coven* received 5.54 million viewers during the premiere episode *Bitchcraft*[42]

- ❖ *Love & Hip Hop Atlanta* received 5.6 million viewers during the third season premiere episode in May 2014
  - "DEBUT OF "LOVE & HIP HOP: ATLANTA" SEASON 3 PROPELS VH1 TO #1 RANKING AMONG ADULTS 18-49, WOMEN 18-49 AND WOMEN 18-34 IN ITS CABLE TIME SLOT ON MONDAY"[43]

- ❖ *"Bad Bitch,"* the song by French Montana featuring Jeremih has over 39,904,277 views, to date, on YouTube[45]

- ❖ Taz's Angels, an "entertainment" group has over 1 million followers on Instagram and between 36,000-99,000 views per video[44]
  - Taz's Angels is also the creator of *Caviar Blaque, LLC*, creator and e-commerce distributor of the apparel slogan *"Bad Bitches Link Up (BBLU)"*

- ❖ *"Bad Ass Bitches,"* an "entertainment website" has over 800,000 likes and followers on Facebook[46]

- ❖ *"Bad Bitches and Good Weed,"* a "website" on Facebook, has to date, approximately 186,550 likes[47]

- ❖ *"Bad bitches are taking over the world,"* a page on Facebook, has the slogan, *"it's about all types of bitches,"* has to date, over 106,239 likes and over 104,642 followers[48]

- ❖ *"Bitches Who Brunch,"* a lifestyle, food, clothing and travel blog for communities residing in D.C., Chicago and New York, has to date, over 18.1k followers on Twitter[49] and over 32.2k followers on Instagram[50]

Your Personal Purchasing Power (PPP©) is at the core of the supply and demand binary. *Macro Systems* (i.e. retailers, multinational corporations, etc.) continue supplying these "bitch narrative" (i.e. capitalist sexist,) goods and services due to *your* consumer demand.

Think about it this way; with every dollar you spend downloading songs that contain the word "bitch," you directly finance *more* songs to be produced with the term "bitch." With every television show you continue to watch with the "bitch narrative," you drive and increase ratings, which directly tells writers, producers and television companies to create *more* shows with the "bitch" storyline and stereotype. With every YouTube video you view, like and share with the "bitch" and "bad bitch" phraseology, you directly circulate the energy and message that fuels the "culture of bitch." With every Facebook page you like or follow with *"Bad Bitch"* or *"Bitch"* in the title, you directly multiply and expand digital spaces that reinforce attitudes and belief systems that "women are bitches." In essence, *your* dollars and consumer engagement breathes life directly into the existence and perpetuation of the "culture of bitch!"

This prolific and widespread "culture of bitch" was created and continues to be sustained by both people *and* institutions. It is our individual attitudes and belief systems, actions, personal viewership and consumerism that gives rise to and maintains global entities, such as media conglomerates, apparel companies, record labels, food and beverage distributors and book publishing companies that manifest the ideology that "woman is equated with 'bitch.'" Examining this phenomenon further, how did this "woman=bitch" notion occur and what are its historical origins?

CHAPTER 3

Cracking the Code: Words DO Mean Things!

> *Common expressions:* "What a bitch!," "HBIC (Head Bitch In Charge)," "Stop bitchin'," "I'm a bad bitch!" "Resting Bitch Face," "What's up bitches?!," "Basic bitch," "Real bitch"
>
> *Songs:* "She's a bitch," by Missy Elliot; "You know I'm the baddest bitch," by Trina; "Perfect Bitch," by Kanye West
>
> *Organizations:* Bitch Flicks, Bitch Magazine and Bitch Media, a feminist media, independent nonprofit

Bitch. Is there any other word in the North American English language with as many uses, connotations and expressions as this? Let me be more specific: Is there any other word, *non-gender specific*, in the North American English language with as many uses, connotations and expressions as the word "bitch?" Just reflect on that for a moment. In this contemporary era, there isn't another predominantly normalized slur more widely used in virtually every area of our society than this one.

As illustrated in Chapters 1 and 2 of this book, "bitch" has become one of the most predominantly normalized terms within our society due to deeply embedded patriarchal ideologies and beliefs that overtime, become action-based and built into structural practices.

It was also brought to light within this book how this word [bitch] is abundantly present in numerous mass media sources, as well as occurs frequently in conversational exchanges between friends (i.e. *"Hey Bitch!"* as in *"Hey Girl!,"*) but is also used as an insult like, *"Fuck you bitch!* or *"Stupid bitch!,"* during moments of Street Harassment or heated exchanges. Looking at the examples of common expressions, songs, and organizations listed on the previous page, I ask, how can a single word have so many uses, as well as numerous, yet polarizing "meanings?"

In my personal and professional experiences speaking with a multitude of diverse people who use the term "bitch," I have found that most people use this word, and many others, without actually knowing a) its exact meaning and b) where it derives from. This is a common trend I have observed where we [people] use language, engage in holidays, cultural traditions, follow religions and mold our lives completely around social mores without ever once questioning the meaning or origin of it. Ironically, we are less knowledgeable about various social phenomena and the origins of certain words and cultural practices we engage in daily, yet we have greater access to information, literally at our fingertips, at this juncture in our human evolution. How did we get here?

Given that the term "bitch" is highly pervasive in our society and overtime, seeps into our consciousness and daily behaviors, I want you to take a moment to ask yourself these two questions and write your answers on the next page:

1) *"What is the exact definition of "bitch?"*

2) *"What is the historical origin of the word "bitch?"*

How do you feel about your responses? Let me say, if you didn't know the answers, no problem! One of the most profound experiences and greatest gifts we can ever have as human beings is learning and acquiring knowledge. *"Knowledge gives life to the soul; the intrinsic value of knowledge is that you act upon it"* [51]. With these wise words from Imam Ali (599-661 CE,) let us now set forth on a journey that will give life to our souls and later, act upon our new knowledge!

History of "Bitch:" Definition and Cultural Origins

The modern-day word "bitch" derives from the Old Norse term *bikkje or bikkjuna*[52], and the Old English term *bicce,* meaning *female dog*[53]. Scholars, such as Geoffrey Hughes, contend that these words were influenced by Grecco-Roman mythology, including the goddesses of the hunt Artemis in Greek culture and Diana in Roman folklore[54]. Both of these goddesses were often portrayed with one or a pack of dogs in paintings or sculptures and were also shown transforming into dogs themselves. Overtime, the comparison between "woman and dog" evolved into a sex-based slur in Ancient Greece and Rome, "equating women to dogs in heat, sexually depraved beasts who grovel and beg for men,"[55].

It was during the Dark Ages in England, however, that Christian rulers catapulted "bitch" into mass society. Recall for a moment the discussion on the *macro system* Patriarchal Ideologies in Chapter 2. The role of Judeo-Christian dogma was central to the proliferation of patriarchy, which uplifted men in every area of society, while subjugating women. These Christian rulers, all men, tactically leveraged their authority to denounce longstanding faith-based practices where femininity was regarded as sacred and holy. Furthermore, for women who did not cleave to the heterosexist, patriarchal, Christian ideal (i.e. women that were unmarried by choice, outspoken, economically independent and women of nature or medicine women,) the slur "bitch" was a perfect preemptive weapon to a) alienate these women from society and b) drive fear into the minds and hearts of "good Christian followers," to obey God's (i.e. men's) law.

Throughout the 16th and 17th centuries, the term "bitch" was interestingly used primarily towards men to insult his character and position in English society. Below are examples of how the widespread socialization of this word was achieved through literary channels, (i.e. media):

> *Complaynt of Roderyck Mor*, by Henry Brinklow's 1524, *"as chast as a sawt bytch,"*[56] which in contemporary English translates to "as pure as a lustful or lecherous bitch."

> Shakespeare's *Troilus and Cressida,* (1602), *"Thou bitch-wolf's son, canst thou not hear?"* and *King Lear* (1606), [thou] art nothing but the composition of a knave, beggar, coward, pander, and the son and heir of a mongrel bitch.

As Clare Bayley states,

> While the word by itself may have described a female entity, its abusive power at the end of the Middle Ages lied in its application to a man – not only putting him down by calling him a woman, but further dehumanizing by equating him with a dirty female animal[57].

By the 18th century, the term "bitch" was largely used in the original definition, "female dog," as an insult to categorize women of a particular ilk. In the 1920s, English and North American society witnessed an acceleration of the term, specifically as a slur towards women, due to an in-depth classification of the word.

John Farmer's *Slang and its Analogues* (1790) defines "bitch" as[58],

- ladies of accommodating morals
- ladies of more complaisance than virtue
- ladies of easy virtue
- an opprobrious woman

With this clear definition, the slur ["bitch"] became a common "go-to" insult among men that opposed women who didn't behave in a manner that met the social climate, like those that participated in the Women's Suffrage Movement of 1920. Remember, this was an era highlighted by patriarchy and the social mores of "a virtuous woman." The "role" of a woman in this era was relegated to domestic duties within the home as a dutiful wife and mother, typified by attributes like modesty, silence, chastity and never challenging male authority. As a result of the Suffragettes' public, "outspoken" demand for voting equality, these women threatened the aforementioned "status quo" and as a result, their character, humanity, agency and positions in society were stripped away with this single term.

This first wave of feminism, within the United States in particular, ushered in a "reclamation" of the word "bitch" during the 1960s. In an attempt to a) withdraw the power and sexist implications of this term from men and b) promote the characteristics of a "bitch" (i.e. "assertive, strong, independent, stubborn, masculine, egoistic, etc.,") as a badge of honor, feminists began embracing this word openly and without shame. The *Bitch Manifesto*, by Joreen Freeman served as an unapologetic declaration of the new woman, separate from the patriarchal, male-centered ideologies of femininity.

Joreen Freeman explicitly contends,

1) *Personality: A Bitch takes shit from no one. You may not like her, but you cannot ignore her.*

2) *Physical. Bitches are big, tall, strong, large, loud, brash, harsh, awkward, clumsy, sprawling, strident, ugly...They clomp up stairs, stride when they walk and don't worry about where they put their legs when they sit. They have loud voices and often use them...Bitches are not pretty.*

3) *Orientation. Bitches seek their identity strictly thru themselves and what they do. They are subjects, not*

> objects. They may have a relationship with a person or organization, but they never marry anyone or anything; man, mansion, or movement. Thus Bitches prefer to plan their own lives rather than live from day to day, action to action, or person to person. They are independent cusses and believe they are capable of doing anything they damn well want to. If something gets in their way; well, that's why they become Bitches.
>
> 4) *A true Bitch is self-determined, but the term "bitch" is usually applied with less discrimination. It is a popular derogation to put down uppity women that was created by man and adopted by women...BITCH does not use this word in the negative sense. A woman should be proud to declare she is a Bitch, because Bitch is Beautiful*[59].

Having been socially, politically and economically silenced, forced into the shadows and oppressed for centuries, this brazen assertion was embraced and adopted by women in droves, which catapulted "bitch" into mainstream society. Over the next 40 years as feminist ideology rose and pierced male-dominated, sexist sociocultural and political spaces, "bitch," while still used as a slur, became widely acceptable, largely due to the influential power of the *macro system,* Media.

Songs, like *"I'm a Bitch,"* by Meredith Brooks in 1997 and *"Da Baddest Bitch,"* by Trina in 2000, dialogue in popular culture television shows such as *Sex and the City* and publications like *Bitch Magazine* furthered the contemporary definition of "bitch" yielding the phenomena we now face..."the culture of bitch."

While this term has been transformed into numerous iterations and is presently accepted in society, the fact still remains that, at the core of the word "bitch" lies a historical energy riddled with sexism and an anti-womanist mission that literally birthed the term into existence! Tracing the origins of this term reveals that, despite unceasing attempts to normalize it via mass media marketing and sociocultural "reappropriation" in this contemporary era, it ["bitch"] was intentionally created as a gender-based slur and therefore, it remains as such.

CHAPTER 4

SHATTERING THE ILLUSIONS:
Breaking BITCH Down!

Throughout this book, we've reviewed the widespread epidemic that is the "culture of bitch" and have identified the numerous sources that have given rise to its proliferation.
The historical origins of "bitch" reveal the stark truth that, in spite of a 50-year campaign to "reclaim" the term as a title of power, 1) "bitch" was unequivocally born out of a patriarchal agenda to defame the totality of women and 2) its usage as a gender-based weapon still thrives in sociocultural, political and public spaces. Moreover, the synergetic relationship between the *macro* and *micro systems* have directly impacted the influential power of the dominant mechanisms of mass media (i.e. visual and auditory media sources, literature, apparel and alcoholic beverages,) which has in turn normalized the term "bitch" within our current era,

making it more palatable for our society to swallow and ingest.

Even with its clear definition and undeniable gender-specific dehumanizing implications, people, communities and institutions remain steadfast in their usage of this term.

As illustrated in Chapter 3, the definition of "bitch" has evolved into numerous colloquial characterizations due to the emergence and influence of the feminist movement of the 1960s, yielding a "lens of empowerment" to the term. It was this segment of feminism that inspired the present-day shift towards "reappropriating" "bitch" as an empowered term, like "*bad bitch.*" However, as exemplified in Chapter 1 with the scripted content of several popular television shows like *How to Get Away With Murder, American Horror Story and Scandal,* and examined in Chapter 2 regarding Street Harassment, the primary motive to employ "bitch" as a defamatory moniker far outweighs any intent to "reclaim" it as an affirmative epithet.

So what do people *really* mean when they use the term "bitch" when referring to a woman? Moreover, because this term has become a common vernacular within our society when speaking about men as well, what is it that people *really* mean when they call a man a "bitch?" Lastly, the term "bitch" is also used to describe an unpleasant situation, as in *"these quarterly reports are going to be a bitch to complete!"* Therefore I ask, what do people *truly* mean when they use "bitch" in this manner?

Let's examine the core, fundamental meanings behind people's implications when they utter this word:

Deconstructing a Social Construct

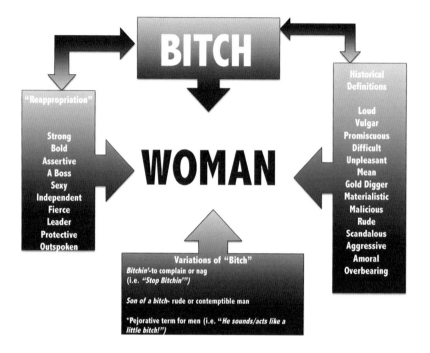

Source: J.R. Baker-Flowers

Take a look at the diagram above. Do you notice any common trends about the deeper implications of the term "bitch?" If so, list your observations on the following page:

_____
_____
_____
_____
_____
_____
_____
_____
_____
_____

So let's break "bitch" down!:

A. When a woman is called a "bitch," the sentiment is generally that she is:

- ⇒ difficult
- ⇒ mean
- ⇒ aggressive
- ⇒ loud
- ⇒ abrasive
- ⇒ scandalous
- ⇒ unpleasant
- ⇒ rude
- ⇒ controlling

Translation: this woman is "out of line," uncontrollable and challenging to "handle."

Common expressions like, *"she's such a bitch!,"* *"what a mean bitch!,"* *"that bitch is crazy!,"* *"Ugh, this bitch!,"* *"fuck that bitch!"* and *"I hate working with that bitch!,"* all reflect the intention to besmirch the character of a woman who isn't *"tam-*

able," "demure," "agreeable," "likable," etc.

Isn't it interesting though that when a man acts in a "rude," "abrasive," "aggressive," "mean" or "scandalous" manner, he's not referred to as "bitch," but rather simply, a man? In other occurrences, he is referred to in the *actual* behavioral trait, (i.e. "*rude, abrasive, aggressive, mean, etc.,*") he has displayed.

B. When a man is called a "bitch," the deeper insinuation is a demeaning code for **"*woman.*"** With statements, like "*he acts like a little bitch!,*" "*he sounds like a bitch!,*" and "*man stop crying like a little bitch!,*" the core implication here is, "*he acts, sounds and behaves in a weak, feminine, girly manner.*"

Translation... "*like a bitch means, like a **woman**.*"

A perfect example of this is a line in the Pilot episode of the 2017 television show, *Shots Fired* where Sanaa Lathan's character, Ashe Akino, is talking with popular football player and brother of the Department of Justice's Prosecutor, Maceo Terry, in a limo. She says to him, "*you sound like a real bitch right now,*" after he heeds with caution to her sexual advances.

> ➢ NOTE: This is also true for other gender-based pejorative terms like "*pussy.*" Take a moment to reflect on this: when someone says, "*don't be a pussy,*" or "*he acts like a little pussy,*" what they're truly saying is "*don't be or act like a vagina,*" which is coded language for "*woman.*"

C. When someone utters the phrase, "*stop bitchin',*" what they're actually saying is "*stop complaining or nagging like a woman.*"

D. When someone uses the term "bitch" in regards to an unpleasant situation, as in "*this is gonna be a bitch to fix,*" or "*ain't that a bitch?!,*" what they're truly saying is, "*this situation or *experience is as difficult and unpleasant as a woman."*

At the center of the word "bitch" lies deeply rooted, fundamentally anti-womanist intimations. Sexism and the total objectification of women have become so normalized and entrenched within this society that the term "bitch" has become a quick, easily accessible verbal shorthand for *"woman."* Why is this?

As explicitly discussed throughout this book and in detail in Chapter 2, Patriarchal Ideologies, endorsed primarily through religion and filtered through mass media sources, have espoused and institutionally implanted fundamentalist philosophies that being born a woman symbolizes a) an inherent inferiority, b) a biological deficiency, c) immorality and d) a predetermined destiny to be led by one's male counterparts. In essence, to be a woman is the least desirable position in humanity!

Reappropriation: The Tool of False Power

Over the last fifty years and more progressively, twenty years, the word "bitch" has been given numerous "favorable" qualities by many feminists and non-feminist identified women in an attempt to overturn enduring male-centered chauvinist definitions of the term. Substantiated by both visual representations, as well as auditory and inscribed dialogue in films, television programs, music and advertisements, the new version of "bitch" denotes a *woman* who possesses qualities of:

- Power
- Independence
- Leadership
- Bravery
- Assertiveness
- Fearlessness
- Sexual prowess
- Strength

But here's why the system of "reappropriation" is inherently faulty:

A. To "reappropriate" or the act of "reappropriation" means to reclaim. "Reappropriation" is a cultural process where a group or community reclaims terms or artifacts that were previously used in pejorative or oppressive ways[60]. The problem with "reappropriating" a slur, like "bitch," is:

   a. A person or group cannot truly own something they did not create

   b. Each time a person, group, or you utters the term "bitch," the sexist, patriarchal and oppressive energy, intention and mindset of the men that designed the word to repress the spirits, bodies and identities of women is resurrected

B. Affirmative language is never confusing, nor does it waver in its authentic ability to uplift and sustainably empower those who both speak and receive it. For example, if someone calls you a *"queen," "warrior," "fierce leader," "strong," "dynamic," "fearless," "radiant," "beautiful"* and/or *"intelligent,"* do you feel confused, upset, enraged or disempowered by their meaning?

C. The word "bitch" instantly dehumanizes a woman's humanity and strips away who she is as a living being/a person, while simultaneously animalizing her into a wild creature

D. Each time a person or you says the word "bitch," there are more spaces directly created for women to be called "bitches" regardless of the implication

E. When someone is called a "bitch," there's an instantaneous mental and physical chain reaction that occurs within them;

    a. an immediate moment of confusion, anger and outrage occurs and the experience is replayed on an unending loop in the person's mind

    b. the person's body shrinks, constricts and becomes smaller due to the energetic vibrations of this slur; (the power of language and the energetic vibrations of words will be discussed in greater detail in Chapter 5!)

F. "Bitch" has become a weaponized tool in the arsenal of Street Harassers to incite fear, public ridicule and embarrassment towards women who ignore and outwardly rebuff the myriad sexist advances they encounter.

> *"It is the psychological condition of those from historically oppressed groups to rationalize their use of slurs as an act of "reappropriation" without understanding that, the very nature of "reappropriation" itself is born out of a system fundamentally designed to enslave them! TRUE power is reclaimed through the creation of terms that uplift, empower and reflects one's divine humanity"*[61].
> -Jamekaa Richelle Baker-Flowers

When we go beyond the surface of words and normalized colloquial vernacular like "bitch," we discover that there are deep-seated painful, repressive and bigoted messages that when spoken, further erase and silence the humanity of women. Words and language are *the* most powerful tools of communication we possess. Why then do we choose to settle for regurgitated, corrupted titles, which we then use to adorn our identities? When we "reappropriate" demeaning, hateful and intentionally sexist dogmatic language, we don't liberate ourselves from our oppressors, but instead, reinvent the wheel of oppression and indirectly join forces *with* them.

To truly transform a society and with it, one's reality, one must first understand the power within their words, for they are the source of all creation!

Part 2:
THE BREAKTHROUGH

CHAPTER 5

Breaking Free:

Your Words Create and Define Your World

"Words are like bullets; if they escape, you can't catch them again" - **Wolof proverb**[62]

"Words are, of course, the most powerful drug used by mankind," - **Rudyard Kipling**[63]

"Carefully watch your thoughts, for they become your words. Manage and watch your words, for they will become your actions. Consider and judge your actions, for they have become your habits. Acknowledge and watch your habits, for they shall become your values. Understand and embrace your values, for they become your destiny," - **Mahatma Gandhi**[64]

"Without knowing the force of words, it is impossible to know more" - **Confucius**[65]

"The limits of my language means the limits of my world" - **Ludwig Wittgenstein**[66]

"The pen is mightier than the sword, but the tongue is mightier than them both put together" - **Marcus Garvey**[68]

> *"There is something about words. In expert hands, manipulated deftly, they take you prisoner. Wind themselves around your limbs like spider silk, and when you are so enthralled you cannot move, they pierce your skin, enter your blood, numb your thoughts. Inside you they work their magic"*-
> **Diane Setterfield**[67]
>
> *"Good words are food, bad words poison"* -
> **Malagasy Proverb**[69]

Across cultures, time and geographic location, our diverse human experiences have been linked through parallel reflections on the quality, content and impact of our words. Why? Language, whether spoken, written, signed or pictogram, is the greatest tool we have that allows us to express ourselves, connect with others, build a civilization or community, inspire sociopolitical movements and continuously unite generations of the past to descendants of the present and future.

Words contain an undeniable power that can shake us to our very core, provoke us to act on lingering desires, elicit emotional responses such as laughter, tears of joy or sadness and even stir up memories long forgotten. Think now about a time when you watched a film, read a poem, heard a speech or lecture, listened to a song or read a book that "spoke to you." Do you recall that feeling of being deeply moved, motivated, elated, upset, reminiscent and/or hopeful? Ask yourself, *"what was it that made me feel this way?"* How one receives and interprets the content of the above mentioned elements may vary from one person to the next, however, the shared agreement is, it is the *words* from these sources that captivate the viewer or listener and triggers such memorable reactions.

Throughout this book, the power and impact of the word "bitch" has been discussed in considerable detail. This term has literally inspired an entire narrative and dominant character featured in an overwhelming percentage of television shows, films, song lyrics and other media sources. Also, the word "bitch" has erected clothing businesses, stimulated alcoholic beverage companies and also inspired many to author books, including myself. Simply uttering the term has 1) motivated shifts in our global society where women have created sociopolitical movements in opposition to Patriarchal Ideologies and 2) conjured both advocates and opponents of its usage. How can one word contain such an overwhelming influence on the world we live in so much, that its very existence has reverberated across tens of thousands of years?

Understanding the Power of Language

Energy. Energy is the source of all creation. Progenitor ancestral civilizations identified this [energy] primordial source as *the* code to the existence of everything. In Ancient Kemet, this wisdom-based teaching was called *Atomist Philosophy* and acknowledged around 2400 BC[70]. In Ancient China, *Qi* (pronounced *ch'i* or *chee*,) was documented as the vital life force that flows through the physical body (meridian lines) and the mental body (consciousness,) as early as the Ancient Shang dynasty (1766-1154 BC) and the Chou dynasty and the Warring States periods (1100-221 BC)[71]. In Ancient India, the first references to *prana,* the cosmic life force, appeared during the 5th and 2nd century BCE[72].

As greater achievements in science emerged, most notably in Quantum and Astrophysics, scholars identified the atom as the source of energy and "the fundamental building unit of each substance"[73]. Within each cell of an organism lies an atom and deeper inside the atom, "there is nothing there – just energy waves...an atom is actually an invisible force field, ...which emits waves of electrical energy"[71]. Regardless of the terminology, *energy* has long been recognized as the fundamental source to all existence, including the essence of the infinite universe. Stay with me here because we're about to go much deeper!

Since energy is *the* foundation or code for all creation, everything is linked through this *shared* source. The aforementioned ancient teachings regarding life energy have been backed by scientists who have further contended that, the cellular and molecular structure of animals, plants, the elements of earth, air, fire, water, minerals and human beings are parallel or connected. Moreover, the universe in which we reside also mirrors the physical and energetic makeup of diverse forms of life, including people. "Humans and their galaxy have about 97 percent of the same kind of atoms"[75] and "each atom has its own distinct frequency, or *vibration*"[76]. Nikola Tesla's groundbreaking research furthered the understanding that the universe is a sea of energy and this energy continuously and simultaneously flows a) to us [humans], b) through us and c) from us impacting every single being and element around us[77].

Given that everything…EVERYTHING is energy and all things are connected through fields or vibrations, it goes without saying that we, human beings, are thus, pure energy. Hence, everything we absorb *and* emit contains energetic vibrations that impact a) the energy within us and b) the energy around us. The same is true regarding our thoughts, emotions, actions and words, which are also forms of energy. Regarding words, "all animals and plants communicate through vibrations"[78]. Therefore, each word that emanates from us transforms into vibrations that can be used to direct energy and shape reality.

In the 1990s, Dr. Masaru Emoto conducted pioneering research on the impact human consciousness, vibrations, emotional energies and words have on the molecular structure of water. Conducting a series of experiments on water prior to and after the exposure to prayer, music and various words spoken to and pasted on the containers, Dr. Emoto froze these water samples and took high-speed photos of the transformations. The water samples that received positive or high vibrating words, such as "gratitude," "love," "joy" and "peace" formed beautiful crystalline structures, whereas the water samples that received negative or low vibrating words like "I hate you," "you make me sick" and "I will kill you," developed shapeless, unsightly structures[79].

Reflect on this: given that the human body is comprised of 60-70% water[80], what do you think the impact of the words *you* think, speak, read, hear and listen to sonically have on the totality of your energetic being (i.e. your body, mind, mood, etc.)?

Contemplating back to Chapter 1 of this book pertaining to our society's voracious consumption of visual, auditory and literary media and Chapter 2 regarding the sources that impact the formation of our attitudes and belief systems, we must understand that what we consume, we become. Literally! Remember, we live in a world and universe comprised of vibrational energy and those vibrations attract like or similar energies or frequencies. Regarding the energy of words, they seep into your consciousness, reverberate throughout your mental, physical, cellular and emotional bodies, you internalize those energetic vibrations and that energy in turn, manifests in your behaviors, thought patterns, content of your language, your internal dialogue and ultimately frames the structure of your daily experiences.

Review the two interactive activities on the next pages that exemplify this point:

Activity 1:

STEP 1: First, allow your eyes to glance upon the list of low vibrating words below. Reflect for a moment how the words feel *within* you. Then, either a) say each word to yourself quietly in your mind or b) say each word aloud. How do you feel when you say or think about each word? Write down your *immediate* reaction in response to each of the words below.

Sad
Angry
Useless
Unworthy
Murder
Sick
Poor
Narcissist
Lack
Rude
Slut
Stupid
Unhappy
Bitch
Ugly
Hate

List your *immediate* reactions here:

_____
_____
_____
_____

_____
_____
_____
_____
_____
_____

STEP 2: Go to a mirror and say each word below *aloud*. As you say each word aloud, observe your facial expressions and body language. Take your time reading each word and REALLY look at the natural reactions on your face and in your body.

Sad
Angry
Useless
Unworthy
Murder
Sick
Poor
Narcissist
Lack
Rude
Slut
Stupid
Unhappy
Bitch
Ugly
Hate

Do you notice any changes in your facial expressions and/or physical reactions? If so, what were your reactions? List them below:

_____
_____
_____
_____
_____
_____
_____
_____
_____
_____
_____
_____
_____

Take a minute to reflect on how you feel and how your mood shifts after saying these words. Feel free to close your eyes and sit quietly for 1-2 minutes during this reflection.

Activity 2:

STEP 1: First, allow your eyes to glance upon the list of high vibrating words below. Reflect for a moment how the words feel *within* you. Then, either a) say each word to yourself quietly in your mind or b) say each word aloud. How do you feel when you say or think about each of the words below? Write down your *immediate* reaction in response to each of the words below.

Happiness
Freedom
Joy
Laughter
Love
Kindness
Peace
Unity
Friendship
Smile
Beautiful
Sisterhood
Human Being
Queen
Boundless
Gratitude

List your *immediate* reactions here:

_____
_____
_____
_____

STEP 2: Go to a mirror and say each word below *aloud*. As you say each word aloud, observe your facial expressions and body language. Take your time reading each word and REALLY look at the natural reactions on your face and in your body.

Happiness
Freedom
Joy
Laughter
Love
Kindness
Peace
Unity
Friendship
Smile
Beautiful
Sisterhood
Human Being
Queen
Boundless
Gratitude

Do you notice any changes in your facial expressions and/or body? If so, what were your reactions? List them below:

_____
_____
_____
_____
_____
_____
_____
_____
_____
_____

Take a moment to reflect on how you feel and how your mood shifts after saying these words. Feel free to close your eyes and sit quietly for 1-2 minutes during this reflection.

If you noticed any differences in your mind, body and overall mood while engaging in the previous activities, you'll understand that words possess an undeniably fundamental energetic vibration and impact on your entire being. In the first activity when you uttered the word "bitch," did you observe or notice similar reactions in your body and/or facial expressions? Examples of your reactions may have included 1) your body immediately constricted, shrunk or became smaller or 2) a slight or pronounced frown or look of disgust immediately appeared across your face, when you said the words "stupid," "hate" or "unworthy?" If so, why do you think you experienced the same or similar reactions when saying these different words?

Write your reflection below:

_____
_____
_____
_____
_____
_____
_____
_____
_____
_____
_____
_____
_____
_____

As stated before, words are simply energy and energy vibrates along an unending spectrum of contraction and expansion (i.e. low and high.) Take a moment to review the energy vibration scale diagrams below and on the following page:

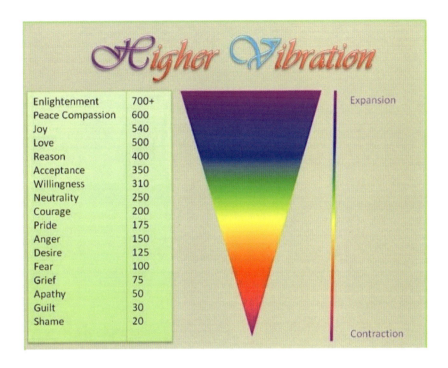

Source: https://www.pinterest.com/

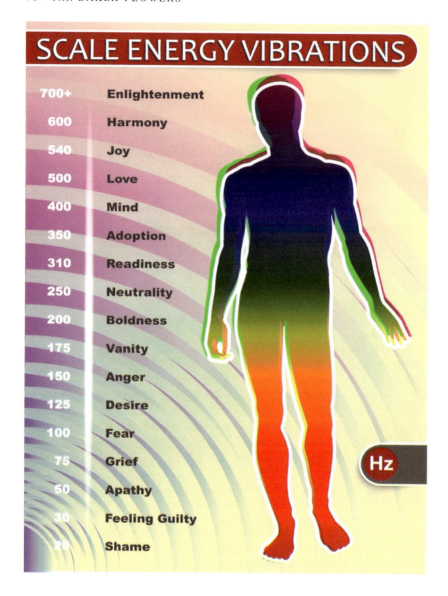

Source: https://www.dreamstime.com

The vibrational scale or spectrum of energy highlights the connection between emotions and corresponding energy. Words [which are energy] reflect the equivalent energetic emotional responses.

In Activity 1, you read the words "angry," "hate," "fear," "sad," "unworthy," etc. These words correspond with the *low vibrational energies* on the spectrum and when spoken aloud or said internally, your body and mind respond in a comparable manner, such as a frown or furrowed brow on your face, your chest lowers or becomes concave, mirroring a contraction and/or you feel your heart racing and body begin to heat up, which is a natural biological response to perceived danger or fear. Similarly, the energy of the word "bitch," is parallel to that of the aforementioned *low vibrational energies.*

As discussed earlier throughout this book, the term "bitch" is predominantly used to belittle, silence and even harm someone, mainly women, who are viewed as "a problem," "less than," or "too much." The sole intention to demean and harm a woman by using this weaponized term indisputably reflects the energies of *hatred, rage, revenge, discouragement, fear, pride, pessimism* and *blame* on the energetic vibrational scale. And as illustrated in Chapter 4, despite our society's ongoing quest to rationalize the usage of "bitch" as an empowering term (i.e. "reappropration,") the inherent *disempowering* energetic historical origins of this term underscores how this attempt is, has always been and will always be fruitless.

In contrast to Activity 1, you read the words "love," "happy," "gratitude," "beautiful," "smile" and "peace" in Activity 2. These words, (love, gratitude and peace,) reflect the *higher vibrational energies* on the spectrum and when you initially glanced at these words and then read them, your body, mind, and entire being most likely experienced an openness where your chest lifted and your shoulders reached back. Additionally, you may have likely experienced a smile appear across your lips, a calmness occurred throughout your body and your heartbeat lowered or became more rhythmic.

These words, as well as the others on the list in Activity 2, (i.e. "queen" and "sisterhood,") resonate with the vibrational energies of *joy, love, empowerment, compassion, freedom* and *harmony*.

Imagine emitting these high vibrating energies to yourself and the people around you through words such as "sister," "beautiful," "person," "friend," "love," etc., rather than the word "bitch" or any of its numerous variations. In speaking through a ***high vibrational frequency***, you emit a sea of positive waves of energy that expand outward and touch every single person and living being around you! Consequently, that ***high vibrating energy*** is returned to you because your ***frequency attracts likeness***. Discussed previously, it has been scientifically proven that sound is a form of energy that contains power and predictable effects on our energetic centers (i.e. chakras, meridian lines,) physical body (i.e. heart, digestive system, liver, brain), and psyche. Therefore, when you consistently consume or view energetic frequencies through television programs, films, music, literary materials, clothing and various commodities containing the term "bitch," you literally draw in, absorb and ***attract*** the sexist and patriarchal energies of this word's historical origins, its intentions *and* meaning! As a result, "bitch" literally becomes a part of you and in exchange, you both house the ***low vibrational energies*** of this word within yourself *and* transmit the low vibrations of the word "bitch" to other energetic beings around you.

The people you attract in your life, your topics of conversation, content of your language, hobbies, interests and your day-to-day experiences reflect your energetic frequencies, which literally shape and form the world we all live in. Furthermore, if you identify with the word "bitch" by labeling yourself as *"a bitch," "a bad bitch," "queen bitch," "head bitch in charge,"* and any other version of this term, the ***low vibrating energies*** of this word will unquestionably produce a constant wave within and from you of the inherent energies of *pride, fear, disempowerment, anger, grief, apathy, shame* and *doubt*.

The words you think and speak create the script to your life's story. Your internal dialogue becomes your external mantra and this ultimately becomes the lines on the page that is your life's screenplay. So ask yourself, are you writing the greatest, most inspiring, abundant, happy, adventurous, boundless love story ever told, or are you writing a recurring horror story?

We must begin to see ourselves as a fundamental part of this world and an integral piece of this vast energetic plane, rather than separate from it. *WE* are responsible for the way our society, communities and world is and has become. Therefore, we must be cognizant of the energies (i.e. thoughts, words and actions) we *individually* cast out into the ethers of space around us, as well as be mindful of the low vibrating energies we consume. In sum, if your frequency is set to "bitch," it's time to change the channel!

CHAPTER 6

Breaking-up With BITCH

Well, here we are! We've journeyed across the terrain of the "culture of bitch" and identified the interconnected *macro* and *micro systems* that fuel this phenomenon. We've traveled back in time to the historical birthplace and evolution of the word "bitch" and deciphered the hidden, patriarchal messages of this verbal enigma. Finally, we've traversed the energetic and vibrational plane highlighting the profound impact our words have on the symbiotic relationship between our internal world and the outer world.

"So what now?" That's what you're thinking right? How do you take all of this information and consolidate it in a useful, deeply transformative and logical way to overturn this repressive phenomenon and more importantly, ignite much needed change in *your* life and throughout society? Like the influential social movements of our society's past, widespread change must always begin within!

Reclaiming Your Truth: A New Era

"Their screams echo, like raging gunshots at each other. Their stares, colder than icy daggers, pierce the very hearts to which they once made loving promises. The utterances from their voices overflow with violent commitments, paradoxical to their recent affectionate devotions."

"There they stand in opposition; the dividing line drawn in the sand, like soldiers at war. They vow never to return to each other, as they've done countless times before. But soon, find themselves once again swept up in the intoxicating aroma of belonging, power, control and the other's embrace."

"This pair's emotional pendulum, vacillating between separation and connection, illustrates their descent into destruction and the erasure of their true nature."

What thoughts entered your mind just now while reading the story above? You may have thought, *"Wow! This couple is SO damaged!"* or *"Why do they stay together? They should just break-up!"* Well, like an intensely toxic relationship, our [society's] love affair with "bitch" has been and is identical to this story...violent, codependent, possessive, diminishing, unhealthy, disempowering and has created a distorted identity. As with any unhealthy relationship, there comes a time when the chains must be severed and the dead branches of the decaying tree must be amputated. The time has come for you to finally end *your* toxic relationship and break-up with "bitch!"

Throughout this book, *BREAKING BITCH: Dismantling the LIES to Reclaim Your TRUTH*, the primary message has been to shed light on the "culture of bitch" and expose how this system of oppression has been designed to normalize patriarchy and weaponize language against women, thus enslaving our society at-large to its coils. The standardization of the "culture of bitch" has elicited a) the rationalization of its personal usage among women through "reappropriation," b) a monolithic mass media production of its colloquial vernacular and c) an all-encompassing desensitized reaction to its utterance.

The minds, behaviors, bodies, interests and energetic centers of every member of our society has been unequivocally saturated with this term's negativity so much, that our identities rest on either being "a bitch" or solely identifying women as "bitches." As an unfortunate result, we have swallowed, ingested and internalized this term's sexist, violent, chauvinist and dehumanizing propaganda. In short, our society has absorbed the lie that is "bitch" and become its slave!

In Chapter 4, it was revealed that "bitch" was designed to silence and repress the inherent sacred power and fortitude that lies within women. It was also illustrated in Chapter 5 that when using the term "bitch," in any manner, you draw into your life the identical oppressive and dehumanizing energetic vibrations this word inherently possesses. Therefore, to hold this word as a source of identity is to suppress, limit and kill the very essence that makes you, *you*! How then can you begin to reclaim your *true* nature and identity in a world hell-bent on tearing you apart from it?

On the following pages are **two** powerfully transformative programs that can support you on your long awaited journey towards freedom, liberation and healing and lead you to your most authentic self!

Allow me to note that these transformative programs are not prescriptive in any manner, nor were they designed to a) cast judgment, b) make you feel inferior or c) promote self-criticism within you for thinking, saying and/or identifying with the word "bitch" at any point in your life.

These activities were designed as tools and techniques to spark your inner awakening through mindfulness and a) ignite your curiosity around your attachment(s) to the word "bitch," b) inquire and contemplate the origins of your experience(s) that influenced or conditioned your mind to embrace the term "bitch," c) evaluate the content of your inner dialogue, as well as the frequency of the word "bitch"---and other disparaging or negative words,---you use to and about yourself and others, d) document the quality and quantity of media you regularly engage with that contain the term "bitch," e) examine the nature of the friendships and connections you have that impact the content of your language and f) encourage you to embrace unquestionably affirmative, positive, loving, kind and encouraging language into your mind, heart, body and spirit.

While I deeply believe these introspective activities are transformative and will support you on your journey towards reclaiming your truth by dismantling the lies you've been conditioned to adopt---without question or opposition---about "bitch," I will affirm that these activities are not *the* way, but simply *a* way. There are an infinite number of approaches to self-liberation, unlearning internalized oppression and releasing oneself from the diverse forms tyranny and subsequent healing. These are two approaches of that infinite number.

> NOTE: Self-transformation/self-liberation is a journey that happens over time, sometimes a lifetime. It is not a race to the finish line, nor will it occur overnight. With self-compassion, dedication, openness, intention and self-acceptance, you inevitably ignite the flame of truth within you and once awakened, your flame can never be extinguished!

ACTIVITY 1:

5-Step Program to Reclaim, Resurrect and Return to YOU!

STEP 1: UNLEARN EVERYTHING & DE-PROGRAM YOUR MIND

From the time you entered into the world in your state of human existence, your psyche began to receive an onslaught of implanted messages from immediate familial ties, members of your neighborhood, teachers, leaders from your religious or faith-based organization, friends, colleagues and associates, which have all impacted your self-image and self-concept.

Recall in Chapter 2, the discussion on how we form our attitudes and belief systems. The above-mentioned constituents have heavily influenced the attitudes and fundamental belief systems you've adopted about yourself and the "roles" of women in this society. Now, let's identify your deeply rooted attitudes and how they came to be.

Trace It Back To The Beginning:

If you identify as a woman, list all the beliefs you have about yourself as a woman (i.e. your "role" in society, your identity, your abilities, strengths, etc.) on the following worksheet. If you identify as a man, gender nonconforming person, etc., please list your beliefs about women on the following worksheet:

This is a free-form exercise so write fluidly what comes to your heart and mind and be honest! Honesty with yourself is the most important tool for transformation!

As a woman, I believe I, or I believe women:

Now, review what you have written regarding your beliefs about women and take a moment to think back to when you first began feeling this way. Write down when you first began agreeing with your attitudes and beliefs *and* list all the sources (i.e. parents, family members, friends, etc.) that have influenced your attitudes:

NOTE: Take your time doing this activity. It is essential to be as thoughtful, honest and accurate as possible. If you need to meditate and think about things over a few days, take your time and come back to it!

My first memories of my beliefs about women are:

Ok, you've identified a) your beliefs and b) from where your beliefs actually derive. Now for the deeper work!

Ask yourself these three questions:

1) *"Do I identify with the word 'bitch?',"* 2) *"Do I view women as 'bitches?'"* and 3) *"Why?"*

Again, BE HONEST WITH YOURSELF!

_____

_____

_____

_____

_____

_____

_____

_____

_____

_____

_____

_____

Finally, ask yourself, *1) "When was the first time I heard the term "bitch?," 2) "When was the first time someone called me a 'bitch?'," and 3) "When was the first time I called someone a 'bitch?'"*

BE HONEST! Honesty leads to freedom and freedom yields change!

_____

_____

_____

_____

_____

_____

_____

_____

_____

_____

_____

_____

How did you feel asking yourself these questions? What themes or memories came up for you? Some memories can be unsettling, infuriating, saddening and very difficult to understand, but know this: a) the road to unlearning deep-seated beliefs and overturning habits is and will be difficult, b) the journey is a challenging one, but the experience along the way allows us to meet our higher and true selves and c) growth can be painful, but like the snake sheds its skin to release the old, we must do the same to embrace the new!

In doing these *"Trace It Back To The Beginning"* activities, the goal is to encourage you to unearth the origins of your belief systems and its influencers in relation to your own self-image, how you view women and the language you use to describe women and/or yourself. The goal here is for you to realize that ***THESE BELIEFS ARE NOT YOUR OWN!*** They are the slanted, biased, ill-informed, and negative views of people who have *also* been socialized and conditioned with this identical destructive narrative.

Journal Exercise:

To facilitate your continual growth and expansion, feel free to use a personal journal regularly to ask yourself the essential questions, *"Who, What, When, Why and How"* you acquired these attitudes. Every time you see limiting beliefs arise in your mind and each time the word "bitch" emerges in your mind and from your mouth, write it down in your journal and say to yourself or aloud, *"this is not my true voice!"*

REMEMBER: Don't judge or blame yourself for your thoughts! Simply a) acknowledge their presence, b) trace their origins, c) repeat to yourself, *"this is not my true voice!"* and d) let it go!

STEP 2: STOP CONSUMING DEATH!

Due to the advancements in technology and media, our minds have become ongoing hamster wheels, both receiving and downloading an unending stream of toxic, sexist, patriarchal and stereotypical images, as well as verbal messages disseminated through television programs, films, social media, music and advertisements. All of these mass media sources have directly coaxed and urged you to *"look, think, behave, dress, speak, walk, eat and have sex like"* the fabricated characters featured in these sources, which were designed to promote an idea---that is not your own--- to persuade you to purchase products solely for the capitalist gain of various *macro systems*.

As discussed in Chapter 1, the amount of media consumption within our society is exorbitant! Hundreds of millions of viewers engage in scripted and "reality-based" television programs, as well as films containing the "bitch" narrative. Additionally, hundreds of millions of consumers' Personal Purchasing Power (PPP©) fuels the continuous production of music, apparel, books and social media sites containing the word "bitch." As a result, "bitch" is EVERYWHERE, ALL THE TIME!

"You are what you eat." Many of us have heard of and have used this popular adage right? But, given that we are energy and energy literally shapes the world around us, as well as our realities, the all-encompassing axiom to live by is *"What You Consume, You Become!"* Becoming aware, mindful and cognizant of the energies you consume regularly can yield magnificent strides in your journey towards reclaiming your truth and resurrecting your authenticity.

Am I Becoming What I'm Consuming?:

Use the tables on the next page to catalog a) the types of media you consume daily and weekly and b) the amount of time you spend consuming and engaging with these sources.

Make sure you document all of the media sources that contain the word "bitch" and the number of times you hear or see the word "bitch."

NOTE: Do not judge yourself! Simply take notice of the content you're consuming and absorbing into your life and entire being. This is an activity of self-awareness and self-awareness yields transformation!

	DAYS OF THE WEEK:	Hours of <u>Daily</u> TV Consumption	Hours of <u>Weekly</u> TV Consumption
Television Shows:	MONDAY		
	TUESDAY		
	WEDNESDAY		
	THURSDAY		
	FRIDAY		
	SATURDAY		
	SUNDAY		

MY FAVORITE TELEVISION SHOWS:	NAME OF TELEVISION SHOW:	CONTAINS THE WORD "BITCH?" YES/NO	HOW MANY TIMES IS THE WORD "BITCH" SAID?

	NAME OF MOVIE:	CONTAINS THE WORD "BITCH?" YES/NO	HOW MANY TIMES IS THE WORD "BITCH" SAID?
MY FAVORITE MOVIES:			

MY FAVORITE MUSIC:	SONG/ARTIST:	CONTAINS THE WORD "BITCH?" YES/NO	HOW MANY TIMES IS THE WORD "BITCH" SAID?

LIST ALL CLOTHING, APPAREL, BOOKS, MAGAZINES, BLOGS YOU FREQUENTLY READ AND PODCASTS YOU LISTEN TO CONTAINING THE WORD "BITCH"

STEP 3: SPEAK LIFE INTO YOURSELF!

Recall in Chapter 5 the discussion on the profound impact our words have on both our internal space (i.e. consciousness, emotions, physical and energetic bodies) and the spaces outside of us (i.e. other people, nature, institutions, etc.) The energy, intention and meaning of the words you speak and hear has the ability to either raise you up and liberate you, as well as manifest joy, abundance, power, happiness, love and other high vibrating energies in your life or disempower you and bind you in a cage of negativity.

> ### *Script Your Life!*
>
> Remember, your words literally create the script to your life's story. What are *you* writing into your life everyday? Do you frequently call yourself and/or others a "bitch," "bad bitch," "stupid bitch," "mean bitch," "bitchy" and/or any other version of this term? Do you often say other inherently demeaning, sexist, oppressive or negative/low vibrating words when speaking about yourself?

Establishing mindfulness[7] of your internal dialogue, self-judgments, the content of your words and your outer dialogue can lead to deeper self-awareness and ultimately, grant you greater insight into how you direct your life and impact the world around you with your words.

---

[7] Mindfulness is a state of active, open attention on the present. When you're mindful, you observe your thoughts and feelings from a distance, without judging them as good or bad. Instead of letting your life pass you by, mindfulness means living in the moment and awakening to experience.
https://www.psychologytoday.com/basics/mindfulness

Use the charts on the following pages and take inventory of how you speak to yourself on a daily occurrence. Write the words that you use <u>frequently</u>. *Take your time, be honest, but remember, don't judge yourself! You are an observer of your life, simply watching how you think and speak.*

MONDAY	MY DAILY WORDS	NUMBER OF TIMES I SAY OR THINK OF THESE WORDS

TUESDAY	MY DAILY WORDS	NUMBER OF TIMES I SAY OR THINK OF THESE WORDS

WEDNESDAY	MY DAILY WORDS	NUMBER OF TIMES I SAY OR THINK OF THESE WORDS

THURSDAY	MY DAILY WORDS	NUMBER OF TIMES I SAY OR THINK OF THESE WORDS

FRIDAY	MY DAILY WORDS	NUMBER OF TIMES I SAY OR THINK OF THESE WORDS

SATURDAY	MY DAILY WORDS	NUMBER OF TIMES I SAY OR THINK OF THESE WORDS

SUNDAY	MY DAILY WORDS	NUMBER OF TIMES I SAY OR THINK OF THESE WORDS

STEP 4: YOUR TRIBE REFLECTS YOUR VIBE!

"Show me your friends and I'll show you your future."
-Anonymous

"Be wary of the company you keep, for they are a reflection of who you are, or who you want to be..."
- Kenneth G. Ortiz

"Put a rose in a sack of fish and soon the rose will start to stink too. Be careful of the company you keep."
- His Holiness the 17th Gyalwang Karmapa Ogyen Trinley Dorje

Do you remember hearing "the grown folks" or the elders in your community say repeatedly, *"birds of a feather flock together?"* I can recall them saying these words to us [youth] and stressing its importance vividly. While they had a unique spin on it, their sage insight spoke volumes to the importance of being aware of the people in your inner circle because they'll "rub off on you."

The main people in your life with whom you regularly communicate and engage, (i.e. your friends, family, associates, business colleagues, intimate partner(s), etc.) are a direct reflection of your vibrations and energy you're sending out into the world. Consequently, the energy, mindset, principles, behaviors, value systems and content of language your "tribe" or community of people possess will inevitably be absorbed, adopted and owned by you. The same is true for those in your "tribe" who use the word "bitch," either to you, around you and/or about you.

Introspective Moment[8]:

Take a moment to ask yourself, *"do the people in my life elevate and enhance my life or do they downgrade my life?"*

<u>Important Note:</u> this is not a question about the superficial or materialistic manner in which the people in your life either elevate or diminish it! Far too often, we [society] operate on a *"what can you do for me?"* and a "take, take, take" principle which only furthers a disconnected and selfish energy in our society. It's the quality of your connections, not the quantity of things you can acquire from others!

This question, *"do the people in my life elevate and enhance my life or do they downgrade my life?,"* is to prompt you to dig deeply within yourself and analyze the real nature of the relationships you have in your life and how these connections impact your mind, attitudes, interests, your energy and your life's trajectory.

---

[8] Introspection is the critical examination of one's conscious thoughts, feelings and mental processing to better understand who they are.[81]

Journal Exercise:

Make a list of the top 5-10 people you spend the majority of your time with. This list can include family, friends, colleagues...essentially the people in your life with whom you communicate (i.e. converse in person, via text, phone, etc.) and socialize, (i.e. dinner, movies, parties, brunch, shopping, travel, etc.) regularly.

Next to each person's name, list a) how you met or became associated with this person, b) why you became friends, c) why you remain in each other's lives, (i.e. what keeps you connected to this person,) d) does this person primarily exude positive qualities, (i.e. caring, thoughtful, kind, loving, honest, trustworthy,) or predominantly exude negative traits, (i.e. critical, judgmental, selfish, dishonest, etc.,) e) do you feel supported, uplifted, empowered and safe when you're with this person or do you feel drained, worn out, unsupported, disempowered, etc. when you spend time with this person and f) what kind of language does this person use regularly, (i.e. positive and high vibrating or negative and low vibrating)?

Note: Be honest in your reflection and responses. Truth and honesty with oneself yields revolution, healing and transformation.

If the people in your "tribe" use oppressive, diminishing, negative, inherently sexist and belittling language constantly, you *will* find yourself using that same language, attracting an unending stream of negative experiences and operating on the same low energetic wavelength too! So, do you want to soar and go far or do you want to be lowered into an abyss of stagnation? If you want to be elevated, you have to let go of the things *and* people that weigh you down, including you!

STEP 5: LOVE YOURSELF FULLY AND BOLDLY!

Self-love is not only the best love, it's the ultimate love! Throughout this book, I've spoken at length about the undeniable fact that we all live in a society dominated by *macro systems* that have manufactured a self-hatred movement and culture solely to capitalize off it. Our minds and entire beings are constantly inundated with toxic, chauvinistic and patriarchal fabricated visual images, auditory messages and texts promoting an anti-womanist agenda.

The very books, magazines, films, television programs, apparel companies, social media, and web-based sites that you've purchased and support regularly, have created diverse sources that have disseminated the "bitch," "bad bitch," "queen bitch," "basic bitch," etc. messages to your consciousness, causing you to extinguish your inner light, silence your true voice and erase your authentic identity.

To *1)* **Unlearn Everything and Deprogram Your Mind**, 2) turn off the television, radio, internet and smart phone to **Stop Consuming Death**, 3) **Speak Life Into Yourself** with affirmative, high vibrating terms and 4) create a *Tribe* that mirrors your *Vibe* of elevation is to reclaim and resurrect the very nature that you were born with...Love! Loving yourself exactly as you are is one of the most revolutionary acts you could ever engage in, especially in this world that seeks to rip you further from yourself.

Self-Love Visualization:

Find a quiet space where you won't have distractions of any kind and give yourself 3-5 minutes to complete this activity. Feel free to grab a small notepad or journal to write down your visions after the activity.

Take a few deep, cleansing breaths and center your mind; ponder how you show love to yourself and why you love yourself.

1) *"What do I love about myself?"* (Celebrate your strengths, innate talents and unique skills and acknowledge your areas for growth, but be gentle with yourself. What makes you, YOU!)

_____
_____
_____
_____
_____
_____
_____
_____
_____
_____
_____
_____
_____
_____
_____
_____
_____
_____

2) *"What makes me truly happy?"* (List hobbies, interests, activities, etc. that make you blissful!)

3) *"What makes my heart/spirit/soul/essence sing?"*

4) *"How do I extend love to myself? (i.e. how do you show or surround yourself with diverse representations of love, do you use mantras or affirmations? List them below:)*

ACTIVITY 2:

14-day "I Am" Affirmation Challenge:

"I Am" are the two most powerful words that can ever be thought or spoken[82]. Every time you use the words "I Am," you literally program yourself to think, speak, and behave in a particular manner, while also commanding the energetic, vibrational universe to respond in kind.

If you say to yourself or others, *"I Am a bitch," "I'm a bitch," "I'm being bitchy," "I'm a bad bitch,"* etc., you're tuning and programming your mind and resultant behaviors, as well as experiences along this **low vibrating** wavelength.

Remember: 1) "bitch" is an inherently sexist slur that was designed to erase sacred femininity and ostracize women from society, 2) "bitch" is a destructive narrative used by businesses and media conglomerates purely for capitalist gain and 3) "bitch" is a weaponized term that furthers violence against women during occurrences of Street Harassment. Therefore, it [bitch] is not a truth and most certainly not *your* truth!

14-day "I Am" Affirmation Challenge:

For the next 14 days, choose a new, **high vibrating (inherently positive)** word each day that reflects your true nature. Begin your day after you awaken by saying this mantra either 1) silently to yourself, 2) out loud with your arms expanded or 3) while looking at yourself in the mirror. Repeat your affirmation 5-10 times and take note of how your body absorbs or responds to the affirmation. You can repeat your "I Am" affirmation throughout the day and before bed after you end your day.

(NOTE: this activity also works if you don't use the term "bitch" to describe yourself. It can enhance the connection you have with yourself and elevate your self-image by breaking patterns of negative, judgmental self-talk.)

Use the form on the next page to guide you in this activity. Remember, your words create your reality. So be bold, be creative and be expansive!

Examples: *"I Am Radiant," "I Am Intelligent," "I Am Creative," "I Am Love," "I Am Unique," "I Am Unlimited," "I Am Dynamic."*

"I AM"	
DAY 1	
DAY 2	
DAY 3	
DAY 4	
DAY 5	
DAY 6	
DAY 7	
DAY 8	
DAY 9	
DAY 10	
DAY 11	
DAY 12	
DAY 13	
DAY 14	

CHAPTER 7

Final Remarks

"My philosophy is that not only are you responsible for your life, but doing the best at this moment puts you in the best place for the next moment."- **Oprah Winfrey**

The time has come, my dear radiant and strong friend! The time has come to finally release and liberate yourself from the oppressive clutches of the "culture of bitch." No longer does your path to *you* have to be obstructed by the lie that is "bitch" and no longer should you readily embrace the patriarchy, capitalist sexism, institutional gender oppression and zombie-automaton social acceptance that has bred and continues to perpetuate the evisceration and erasure of women!

For far too long, your identity, your spirit, the very essence of you, has been held hostage, manipulated and stage-managed to accomplish one thing...imprisonment! The repressive institutions that control mass media and the production and distribution of commodities have yielded their collective economic power to feed you an unending stream of lies, all to confine you to their veiled, anti-womanist agenda cloaked in the illusory ideas of "entertainment," "free speech without accountability" and "new age women's empowerment!" These and other systemic tyrants have worked tirelessly to steer you away from harnessing the limitless and abundant power you possess innately. Your life, your power, feeling *empowered* and your unshakable connection to yourself and the entire world around you are non-negotiable! So why lock yourself in a cage when you were born free?

Now, not tomorrow, not next week, NOW is the pivotal moment in your life to stop agreeing to a lesser version of you! NOW is the time to finally and confidently detach your life force from the lecherous smoke-and- mirror distraction that is the "culture of bitch" and awaken and tune-into the primordial voice inside that says, *"Know your truth and BE your truth!"* NOW, as you read these words in this present moment, is the time when you decide to both elevate yourself and in turn, contribute to the progressive elevation of our global society and human evolution or act as a direct participant to the steady decline of humanity and the continual maltreatment of women.

Are you ready to dismantle the wall of lies and oppression that was built to encase you in its shadow of deceit? Are you ready to tear down that tower of babble erected to confuse you and obscure the truth…YOUR truth? Are you ready to break free from the psychological and energetic chains of forced internalized oppression and emerge into your best, most authentic self?

Grab your sledgehammer my powerful friend and let's get to work!

Appendix 1

"Bitch" on Television

"Animal Kingdom" - Tues 05/30/17- Episode-'Eat What U Kill'

"Being Mary Jane" - Tues 7/18/17 - Episode - 'Feeling Raw'; Tues. 7/25/17 - 'Feeling Conflicted'

"black-ish" - Weds 04/26/17- Episode - 'Sister, Sister'; Tues 11/14/17 - 'Don't Feed the Animals'

"Blindspot" - Weds 05/03/17- Episode - 'In Words, Drown I'

"Blue Bloods" - Thurs 6/15/17 – Episodes - 'My Funny Valentine' - First air date - 2/9/11 'Age of Innocence ' - First air date - 2/2/11, Sun 7/2/17 - Episode - ' 'Backstabbers' - First air date - 10/23/15, 'Rush to Judgment' - 10/30/15, 'The Bullitt Mustang' - 11/6/15- Thurs - 7/20/17 - Episode - 'Sins of the Father- Original air date - 1/2/15

"Chicago PD"- 'Grasping for Salvation'-Weds 04-26-17

"Chicago Justice" - Sun 05/07/17 - Episode - 'Fool Me Twice'

"The Carmichael Show" - Weds 06/21/17 - Episode - 'Cynthia's Birthday', Weds 7/5/17-Episode -'Morris'

"The Catch"- Episode - 'The Knock Off', Thurs 04-27-17, Thurs 05/04/17- Episode -'The Cleaner,' Thurs 05/11/17 - Episode - 'The Mockingbird'

"Dish Nation"- Weds 05/03/17, Thurs 05/04/17, Fri 05/05/17, Weds 05/17/17, Weds 05/24/17, Fri 05/26/17, Fri - 06/02/17, Fri 06/09/17, Weds 06/21/17, 6/23/17, Mon - 7/3/17, Weds- 7/5/17,

Thurs- 7/6/17, Mon 7/10/17, Thurs 7/13/17, Fri 7/14/17, Mon- 7/17/17,Thurs-7/20/17, Mon - 7/24/17, Tues – 11/14/17

"Empire" - Weds 05-03-17 - Episode- 'Civil Hands Unclean,' Weds 05/10/17- Episode - 'Absent Child,' Weds 05/17/17- Episode-'Toil & Trouble Part 1'& Weds.05/24/17-'T&T Part 2'

"Greenleaf" -Weds 04/26/17 - Episode - 'Born to Trouble

"Harry"- Fri 05/05/17

"In Living Color" - Episode - 'Anton & The Reporter' - 12/8/91

"Major Crimes"- Episode - 'Penalty Phase '- Sunday 4-23-17

"Late Night with Seth Myers" - Thurs - 7/13/17

"Law & Order"- Sat 7/8/17- Episode -'Personae Non Grata'-First air date-5/14/08; Fri - 7/14/17 - Episode- 'Avatar' - First air date- 9/29/06

"Law & Order: Criminal Intent"- Sun 7/9/17 - Episode - 'Jones' - First air date - 10/21/01; 'The Good Doctor' -11/25/01; 'Enemy Within' - 12/3/01; 'Homo Homini Lupus' - 3/3/02

"Law & Order SVU"-Episode - 'Goliath'-Monday 4-24-17 (First air date 5-24-05); Episode 'Design'- (First air date 9-25-05); Sat. 04/29/17; Episode - 'Hothouse' (First air date-01/13/09); Snatched'-(First air date-02/03/09); Sun. 04-30-17 - Episode 'Transitions'; (First air date-02/10/09); Sat 05/06/17 - Episode - 'Anchor' (First air date-2/9/2000); Sat 05/20/17-Episode-'Totem' & Sat 05/27/17-Episode-'Strange Beauty'-First air date-12/10/12; Sat 6/10/17- Episode- 'Hysteria' - First air date - 10/11/99, 'Wander-lust' - First air date, 10/10/99; 'Stalked' - First air date - 10/19/99; Sat 6/17/17; Noncompliance'- First air date -10/24/2000; 'Asun-der' - First air date - 10/01/2000; 'Taken' - First air date - 12/05/2000; - Fri 6/23/17 Episode-'Parasites' - First air date - 4/27/01; Sat 6/24/17; 'Protection' - First air date - 2/4/02; 'Prodigy'

- First air date - 1/18/02, Sun 6/25/17, 'Quickie' - 2/17/10, 'Savior' - 3/3/10, 'Surrendering Noah' - 5/20/15, Sat 7/1/17, 'Lust' - 10/18/02

'Disappearing Acts' - 10/25/02, 'Dolls' - 11/08/02, 'Juvenile ' - 11/22/02, 'Resilience ' - 12/06/02, 'Night' - 5/3/05, 'Lust '-10/18/02, Sat 7-8-17, 'Dominance' - 4/4/03, 'Fallacy - 4/18/03, 'Soulless' - 5/16/03

"Legends of Chamberlain Heights"- Episode- 'My Father the Zero'-7/30/17; 'Party Over Here, F**k You Over There'-8/6/17; 'Hom*coming' - 8/13/17 'Legends of Lock-Up'- 8/20/17

"Lucifer" - Mon 5/15/17 - 'God Johnson'

"Macgyver"- Fri 7/14/17- Episode- 'Metal Saw' - First air date - 9/30/16

"Major Crimes" - Sun 05/07/17 - Episode - 'Headlight Part 4', Sun 05/14/17 - Episode -"Hindsight #5, Sun 05/21/17 - Episode - 'Medical Causes' - First air date- 8/28/12 -Sun 11/23/17 -Episode - 'Backfire - First air date - 8/12/13

"Marlon" – Weds - 8/16/17- Episode - 'Pilot'

"NCIS: New Orleans" – Tues – 11/14/17 – Episode - 'Sins of the Father'-11/14/17

"NYPD Blue"- Sun. 4/30/17- Episode 'Goodbye Charlie'- (First air date-04/18/2000); Sun 06/11/17- Episodes - 'Cops & Robbers' - First air date - 11/27/01, Sun 7/2/17 - Episode - 'Gypsy Woe's Me' - First air date - 3/26/02

"Queen Sugar"- Tues, 9/6/16- Episode "First Things First," Wed, 6/28/17, "What Do I Care For Morning," Weds - 7/5/17 - 'My Soul's High Song'

"Queen of the South" - Thurs 6/22/17 - Episode - 'Un Pacto con el Diablo'; Thurs 7/6/17 - 'El Nacimiento de Bolivia; Thurs

7/27/17 - Episode - 'Sacar con Si'on de Mar'; Thurs 8/24/17 - Episode - 'Todas las Horas Hieren'

"Rebel" -Tues 3/28/17- Episode - 'Pilot- 'My Brother's Keeper' - 4/4/17

"Rizolli & Isles" - Sun 8/29/17- Episode- 'Cuts Like A Knife'- First air date - 7/24/12

"Rookie Blue" - Sat 7/15/17 - Episode - 'A Little Faith' - First air date - 9/1/11

"Shades of Blue"- Episode - 'Unpaid Debts' Sunday 4-23-17

"Saturday Night Live"- Sat. 04/29/17 (First air date-01/21/17); "Saturday Night Live" - Sat 05/06/17; Sat 05/20/17

"Scandal" - Thurs 05/11/17 - Episode - 'Head Games'

"Shades of Blue" - Sun 04/30/17- Episode - 'Chaos Is Come Again'

"Shots Fired" – 'Pilot – Weds 03/22/17, Weds 05/03/17- Episode, 'Hour Seven: Content of Their Character', Weds 05/10/17 - Episode - 'Hour Eight: 'Rock Bottom', Weds 05/17/17 - Episode - 'Hour Nine: Come to Jesus'

"STAR" – Weds 10/11/17 – Episode - 'FUA.....Good Night'; Weds 10/18/17 - 'It Ain't Over'; Weds 11/8/17 - 'Let The Best Manager Win'; Weds 11/15/17 Faking It

"Tales" - Tues 7/4/17- Episode - "F" The Police - First air date - 6/27/17

"TMZ" - Fri 05/12/17 – (Kelly Osbourne speaking about her book, 'There's No Fucking Secrets: Letters From A Badass Bitch')

"The Brave" - 10/9/17- Episode - 'The Greater Good'

"The Good Doctor" - 'Pilot - Burnt Food' - 9/25/17

"The Mayor" Episode: 'Buyer's Remorse' - 10/17/17

"The Real" - Episode- ' Hit Reply; Manslation; You Be Your Husband', Thurs 4-27-17, Thurs 05/11/17 (At the very end of the show, the hosts plug this week's co-host Kelly Osbourne's book- 'There's No Fucking Secrets: Letters From A Badass Bitch', Thurs. 05/25/17 (Jeannie Mai greets her cast members every morning in her bathrobe by saying *"Good Morning Bitches!"*)

"The Q" - Thurs 6/22/17

"The Tonight Show"- Friday- 6/16/17, Weds -7/12/17 - Amy Poehler, guest & used 'B' word - First air date - 6/20/17

"Wendy" Thurs. 5/25/17; Thurs - 7/20/17

"Zoo"- Thurs 7/6/17- Episode - 'Diaspora

Bibliography

1 http://www.collective-evolution.com/2014/09/27/this-is-the-world-of-quantum-physics-nothing-is-solid-and-everything-is-energy/

2 http://www.statisticbrain.com/television-watching-statistics/

3 http://www.pewinternet.org/2015/10/29/technology-device-ownership-2015/

4 https://www.brandwatch.com/blog/96-amazing-social-media-statistics-and-facts-for-2016/

5 https://www.quantcast.com/bravotv.com#/trafficCard

6 http://womenintvfilm.sdsu.edu/files/2015-16-Boxed-In-Report.pdf

7 http://www.thewrap.com/tv-writing-remains-white-mans-world-writers-guild-study-finds-82556/

8 https://www.statista.com/topics/1639/music/

9 Fox, V. C. (2002). Historical perspectives on violence against women. Journal of International Women's Studies, 4(1), 15-34.

10 Bible, King James Version, Ephesians 5: 22, 23 and 24

11 Fox, V. C. (2002), p. 20

12 http://articles.baltimoresun.com/1998-04-17/news/1998107056_1_rule-of-thumb-phrase-rule-false-etymology

13 http://www.musicworksforyou.com/news-and-charts/news/177-how-our-brains-process-music

14 http://www.hbs.edu/faculty/Publication%20Files/07-037.pdf

15 http://www.unicef.ie/wp-content/themes/iboot-child/micro-sites/itsaboutus/cards/unicef-itsaboutus-gender-sexism.pdf

16 https://newint.org/blog/2014/10/15/feminism-capitalism-equal-pay/

17 http://www.neatorama.com/2008/07/07/who-owns-what-on-television/

18 Seidman, Robert (February 22, 2015). "List of how many homes each cable network is in as of February 2015". *TV by the Numbers.* Zap2it. Retrieved March 14, 2015

19 Goldberg, Lesley (April 8, 2014). "Oxygen Orders Seven New Series, Sets Network Rebranding". *The Hollywood Reporter.* Retrieved April 8, 2014.

20 http://www.stopstreetharassment.org/wp-content/uploads/2013/12/SSH-KnowYourRights-StreetHarassmentandtheLaw-20131.pdf

21 http://www.stopstreetharassment.org/wp-content/uploads/2013/12/SSH-KnowYourRights-StreetHarassmentandtheLaw-20131.pdf

22 http://www.dailymail.co.uk/news/article-3030062/Fury-police-anti-rape-poster-blames-women-allowing-friends-attacked.html

23 http://cargocollective.com/jisoochoi/P-a-a-r

24 Attitudes, Behavior, and Social Practice. Journal of Sociology and Social Welfare. March 2011

https://www.wmich.edu/hhs/newsletters_journals/jssw_institutional/individual_subscribers/38.1.Chaiklin.pdf

25 http://www.nytimes.com/2009/11/14/business/media/14vulgar.html

26 http://www.fcc.gov/eb/oip/

27 http://www.refinery29.com/powerful-women-arent-bitches

28 http://www.statisticbrain.com/television-watching-statistics/

29 https://fusiondotnet.files.wordpress.com/2013/12/ezzell.reclaiming_critical_analysis.pdf

30 https://www.washingtonpost.com/blogs/she-the-people/wp/2014/06/04/new-study-suggests-street-harassment-is-widespread/?utm_term=.43b19597ea1e

31 http://pdfproc.lib.msu.edu/?file=/DMC/African%20Journals/pdfs/social%20development/vol16no2/jsda016002005.pdf

32 http://www.dailymail.co.uk/tvshowbiz/article-3810184/Amber-Rose-lands-8m-meet-greet-world-tour-deal-discuss-sex-love-share-stories-fans.html

33 https://butisitnew.info/2016/11/19/rihannas-bbhmm-becomes-1st-ever-age-restricted-vevo-certified-video/

34 https://www.riaa.com/gold-platinum/?tab_active=default-award&ar=Rihanna&ti=Bitch+Better+Have+My+Money#search_section

35 http://sherryargov.com

36 http://classic.atrl.net/forums/showthread.php?t=323424

37 http://www.statisticbrain.com/nicki-minaj-total-albums-sold/

38 http://www.nytimes.com/2009/04/23/books/23skinny.html

39 https://butisitnew.info/2016/11/19/rihannas-bbhmm-becomes-1st-ever-age-restricted-vevo-certified-video/

40 http://www.nydailynews.com/entertainment/tv/real-housewives-atlanta-tops-sister-shows-ratings-article-1.2136458

41 http://variety.com/2016/tv/news/ratings-abcs-scandal-how-to-get-away-with-murder-fade-thursday-1201710499/

42 http://tvbythenumbers.zap2it.com/sdsdskdh279882992z1/wednesday-cable-ratings-duck-dynasty-beats-american-horror-story-coven-mlb-baseball-bad-ink-south-park-more/208047/

43 http://www.vh1.com/news/133011/love-hip-hop-atlanta-season-3-ratings/

44 https://www.instagram.com/tazsangels_/

45 https://www.youtube.com/watch?v=2yfjYdRWd5E

46 https://www.facebook.com/badass1.official/

47 https://www.facebook.com/RealTeamWeed/

48 https://www.facebook.com/smartkhatri2/

49 https://twitter.com/BtchesWhoBrunch

50 https://www.instagram.com/bitcheswhobrunch/

51 https://www.al-islam.org/articles/various-sayings-imam-ali-ibn-abi-talib-imam-ali-ibn-abu-talib

52 http://www.etymonline.com/index.php?term=bitch

53 http://clarebayley.com/2011/06/bitch-a-history/

54 Hughes, Geoffrey. An Encyclopedia of Swearing: The Social History of Oaths, Profanity, Foul Language and Ethnic Slurs in the English-Speaking World. M.E Sharpe Inc., 2006. The defini-

tion of "Bitch" appears on pages 23 and 24

55 http://clarebayley.com/2011/06/bitch-a-history/

56 Brinkelow, Henry. *Henry Brinklow's Complaynt of Roderick Mors.* London, N. Trubner & Co., 1876.

57 http://clarebayley.com/2011/06/bitch-a-history/

58 https://archive.org/stream/slangitsanalogue01farmuoft#page/4/mode/2up/search/bitch , Farmer, John S. Slang and its Analogues, past and present. Vol. 1-A to Byz. 1790.

59 http://www.jofreeman.com/joreen/bitch.htm

60 http://www.sciencedirect.com/science/article/pii/S0388000110000975

61 Jamekaa Flowers, Founder and Creator of The UNLEARNing Project® https://www.instagram.com/p/uWzSEIR0hk/

62 http://blog.africaimports.com/wordpress/2009/07/african-proverb-about-the-power-of-words/

63 http://www.booksbyhunter.net/?p=1282

64 http://www.azquotes.com/quote/453692

65 http://www.goodreads.com/quotes/tag/power-of-words

66 Ibid. http://www.goodreads.com/quotes/tag/power-of-words

67 Ibid. http://www.goodreads.com/quotes/tag/power-of-words

68 https://www.goodreads.com/author/quotes/28955.Marcus_Garvey

69 http://www.siliconafrica.com/100-african-proverbs-i-always-keep-with-myself/

70 http://africancreationenergy.blogspot.com
http://www.jpanafrican.org/ebooks/eBook%20Stolen%20Legacy.pdf

71 http://www.feeltheqi.com/articles/rc-history.htm

72 Prana: the Universal Life Force, by Swami Satyananda Saraswati, Zinal (Switzerland), September 1981

73 https://www.our-energy.com/atom.html

74 http://www.lifetrainings.com/We-are-made-of-Energy-not-Matter.html

75 http://www.space.com/35276-humans-made-of-stardust-galaxy-life-elements.html

76 http://www.lifetrainings.com/We-are-made-of-Energy-not-Matter.html

77 Michael Talbot and David Bohm, *The Holographic Universe*

78 Ibid, http://www.lifetrainings.com/We-are-made-of-Energy-not-Matter.html

79 Emoto, Masaru, *Hidden Messages in Water*, 2005

80 https://water.usgs.gov/edu/propertyyou.html

81 Schultz, D. P.; Schultz, S. E. (2012). *A history of modern psychology (10th ed.)*. Belmont, CA: Wadsworth, Cengage Learning. pp. 67–77, 88–100. ISBN 978-1-133-31624-4

82 *I Am Discourses*, Godfre' Rae King and Saint Germain, Saint Germain Press, 1940

Index

A
ABC, 15, 22, 23, 33
Activity, 12, 48, 50, 52, 53, 54, 57, 62, 75, 76
Affirmation, 8, 73, 76,
Alcohol, 11, 12, 18, 23, 25, 29, 39, 46
Apparel, 7, 11, 18, 29, 33, 34, 39, 62, 65, 71
    Caviar Blaque Apparel, 11, 18
    One Bad Bitch, 18
Attitudes, 26, 27, 28, 29, 30, 31, 33, 34, 47, 58, 61
Argov, Sherry, 11, 18, 32
Artists, (musicians,) 17
Astrophysics, 46
Audiobook, 12, 32

B
Belief systems, 26, 27, 28, 29, 30, 31, 33, 34, 47, 58, 61
BET, 23
Beyoncè, 11, 18, 32
Bitch, 10, 11, 12, 13, 14, 15, 16, 17, 18,
    Bad bitch, 5, 6, 11, 17, 18, 29, 32, 33, 35, 39, 54, 66, 71, 76
    Historical origins, 36, 37, 38
Bitch Vodka, 11
Bitch Wine, 11
Black lives matter, 6
Bravo, 14, 23
Brooks, Meredith, 11, 17, 38

C
Capitalism, 22
Capitalist, 6, 7, 14, 18, 22, 23, 31, 33, 62, 76, 78
Capitalist Sexism, 20, 22, 23, 25, 78
Catcalling, 23, 29

Caviar Blaque Apparel, 11, 18
CBS and News Corporation, 46
Christianity,
    Christian, 11, 36, 37
Comcast, 23
Confucius 45
Consciousness, 7, 26, 29, 36, 46, 47, 66, 71
Constitution, 24

D
Dr. Dre, 17

E
Energy,
    Vibration and Frequency 7, 32, 33, 38, 46, 47, 52, 53, 54, 62, 68, 69
Emoto, Dr. Masaru, 47

F
Falchuck, Brad, 14
Feminism, 39
Feminist, 16, 38, 39, 42
Fey, Tina, 16
Films, 5, 12, 16, 21, 22, 42, 46, 54, 62, 71
Freedom of speech, 6, 24

G
Gandhi, Mahatma, 45
Garvey, Marcus, 45
Greece, Ancient, 36
Groping, 23, 24, 25, 26, 29

H
Hip Hop, (music,) 17

I
Ice Cube, 17

Individual Attitudes, 7, 26, 29, 34
Immediate familial ties, 26, 27, 28, 30, 58
Introspection, 60
Introspective, 69
Ivana Bitch, 18

J
Judeo-Christian, 20, 21, 36

K
Kipling, Rudyard, 45

L
Leering, 23, 29

M
Macro System, 19, 20, 21, 22, 23, 24, 25, 26, 30, 31, 33, 36, 38, 62, 71
Madonna, 18
Malagasy Proverb, 45
Media, 5, 6, 7, 11, 12, 13, 16, 17, 18, 20, 21, 22, 23, 25, 26, 27, 28, 30, 31, 34, 35, 38, 46, 62, 76
    Media consumption 12, 28, 31, 62, 47
    Mass media, 35, 38, 39, 42, 56, 62, 78
    Media conglomerates, 76
    Social media 6, 12, 21, 28, 31, 62, 71
    Visual, auditory and literary, 39, 47
Micro System, 19, 25, 26, 29, 31, 39, 56
Minaj, Nicki, 17, 18, 32
Movies, 10, 12, 23, 64
Multinational Media Corporations, 22, 23
    ABC, 15, 22, 23, 33
    BET, 23
    Bravo, 14, 23
    CBS and News Corporation, 46
    Comcast, 23
    MTV, 23

NBC, 14, 16, 23
Oxygen, 23
Paramount Pictures, 23
Time Warner, 22
Viacom, 23
VH1, 23, 33
Walt Disney Company, 23
Music, 10, 12, 17, 18, 19, 21, 22, 23, 29, 30, 42, 47, 54, 62, 65
Musicians (artists,) 17
Murphy, Ryan, 14

N
Nas, 11, 17
NBC, 14, 16, 23

O
One Bad Bitch, (apparel,) 18
Oppression, 7, 8, 20, 22, 24, 25, 44, 57, 79

P
Patriarchy, 6, 7, 20, 21, 22, 24, 29, 31, 36, 37, 56, 78
Personal Purchasing Power, (PPP©) 26, 31, 32, 33, 62
Prana, 46

Q
Qi, 46
Quantum (physics,) 46

R
Rap, (music,) 17
Rape, 25
Raging Bitch Ale, 11, 18
Reality television (reality tv,) 5, 10, 13, 14, 62
Reappropriation, 7, 38, 42, 43, 56
Religion, 12, 20, 35, 42
Representation (media,) 5, 6, 16
The Real Housewives, 10, 13, 22, 23, 27, 32

Rihanna, 10, 17, 18, 32
Rhimes, 15, 16
Rock, (music,) 17
Rose, Amber, 11, 18, 32
Rome, Ancient, 36

S
Self-love, 71
Setterfield, Diane, 45
Sexism, 6, 7, 14, 17, 19, 20, 22, 23, 25, 26, 29, 38, 41, 78
Sexual objectification, 23, 41
Snoop Dogg, 17
Street Harassment, 6, 20, 23, 24, 25, 26, 29, 30, 31, 35, 39, 76
Stereotypes, 14, 22, 26, 28

T
Television, 5, 10, 12, 13, 14, 16, 21, 22, 23, 28, 29, 31, 33, 38, 39, 41, 42, 46, 54, 62, 63, 71

U
Universe, 7, 47, 76

V
Vibration, 47, 53, 54, 56, 69, 76
Visualization, 71

W
Weapon, (weaponized,) 37, 39, 43, 54, 56, 76
West, Kanye, 11, 35
Winfrey, Oprah, 78
Wittgenstein, Ludwig, 45
Wolof proverb, 45

Z
Z, Jay, 11

About the Author

J.R. Baker-Flowers (Jamekaa Richelle Baker-Flowers,) is the Founder and Producer of The UNLEARNing Project®, LLC, a social change multimedia initiative designed to create socially transformative media, provide activities and resources to unlearn racism, sexism and homophobia. Under this social change initiative, J.R. Baker-Flowers produced her first documentary in 2014, *"Reverend Dennis W. Wiley: A Journey Towards Inclusiveness,"* which tells the personal story of Dr. Reverend Dennis W. Wiley's voyage towards implementing an affirmative, inclusive and human-centered philosophy within one of the oldest African-American churches in Washington, D.C. Along with his wife, Co-Pastor Reverend Dr. Christine Y. Wiley, PhD, their mission to expand women's rights, implement inclusive practices towards the LGBTQ community and empower historically oppressed groups through humanist Christian education has significantly impacted the lives of residents within the District of Columbia.

In May 2015, J.R. Baker-Flowers received a grant from The Puffin Foundation, Ltd. to independently produce and direct *The Goddess Unbound: No BITCH Here Project©* and in August 2016, this initiative was released to address the socio-institutional crisis that she identified as the rising "culture of bitch." With the increasing sexist and anti-womanist portrayals of women and girls in numerous media sources, *The Goddess Unbound: No BITCH Here Project's©* mission is to 1) bring attention to the pervasive usage of the term "bitch" in sociocultural spaces, films, television programs and social media forums, 2) educate groups and communities on the historical evolution of the word "bitch," as well as deconstruct the definitions of the term and highlight the deeply-rooted patriarchal foundation of "reappropriating" "bitch," and 3) spark sustainable transformation across collective mass media sources to abolish the usage and mass production of the word "bitch."

In 2017, J.R. Baker-Flowers authored her first book, *BREAKING BITCH: Dismantling the LIES to Reclaim Your TRUTH*, to further analyze and deconstruct the intersecting sociopolitical, capitalist, economic, and industrial media mechanisms that have engineered, as well as maintains and profits from the sociocultural and sexist malady that is the "culture of bitch." Additionally, she self-published this book to empower readers through the provision of introspective-mindfulness activities designed to support readers' journeys towards healing internalized subjugated identities, which includes abolishing their usage of the word "bitch," as well as other patriarchal verbiage and alternatively, embrace affirmative terminology and labels towards themselves, women and humanity.

Originally from Atlanta, Georgia, J.R. Baker-Flowers received a Bachelor's of Arts degree in Psychology in 2005 from Clark Atlanta University. After working in nonprofit management serving socioeconomically marginalized low-income youth through the development of educational and holistic resource-driven programs, J.R. Baker-Flowers attended Clark University in Worcester, Massachusetts in 2007 and received a Master's of Arts in Community Development and Planning in 2009.

J.R. Baker-Flowers currently resides in Washington, D.C. leading social change-centered workshops through her initiative, The UNLEARNing Project, LLC®, to highlight the pervasiveness of the word "bitch" in diverse sociocultural, economic and multimedia spaces, while also bringing attention to the structural mechanisms that foster and support learned sexist, racist, homophobic and heterosexist biases and stereotypes.

For updates on her work, please follow J.R. Baker-Flowers at https://jrbaker-flowers.com.

Made in the USA
Columbia, SC
07 March 2018